KITCHENS
HOW TO REALLY FIT YOUR OWN

STEVE LAKE
KITCHEN FITTER

KITCHENS – HOW TO REALLY FIT YOUR OWN 2011

FIRST PUBLISHED 2007 BY RS KITCHENS

2ND EDITION 2011

ISBN 978-0-9557-024-3-3

PRINTED IN ENGLAND

CONTENTS

ADDITIONAL HELP

I hope this book helps to answer all of your questions relating to your kitchen-fitting project. If you discover a subject not covered in the pages of this book please visit the website at

www.diykitchenfitting.co.uk

Additional pages are posted there as well as some common DIY questions concerning kitchens. If an answer cannot be found there please feel free to contact me directly through the website and I will endeavour to provide a solution for you.

1 - INTRODUCTION

Whatever your age or level of experience, this book will prove invaluable to those of you confident enough, but lacking the knowledge and experience to undertake the task of replacing or updating your own kitchen. It is based and written on more than twenty years experience in the domestic kitchen installation business and will supply you with many valuable tips, as well as highlighting some common pitfalls to DIY installations.

The procedures described in this book are intended for self-assembly kitchens consisting of standard cupboards fitted with a laminated worktop available from various kitchen suppliers. However, much of the content and terminology can be applied to any type of kitchen with any type of worktop.

A website to compliment this book is available for use online. It contains a number of procedures that though not common, may be of interest to you while fitting your kitchen. 'How to' pages are available for free download in the same format of this book and can simply be added to relevant section or chapter. The website can be found at diykitchenfitting.co.uk.

This edition has been specifically designed to read before buying your kitchen and also for you to refer to and make notes in while fitting the kitchen. Reading it before starting your project will provide a comprehensive insight into the many and varied tasks and abilities required to successfully install your own kitchen. Using the guide while fitting your kitchen will help you to overcome problems that may arise once the old kitchen has been removed.

The book is intended to use in conjunction with the instructions supplied with your kitchen, it will expand on the basic techniques described within them. Blank spaces and pages are for you to make notes as you go. Once your kitchen is complete you can tuck important instructions at the back of the guide and store it away for future reference either for yourself or for the next owner.

Divided into easy read sections, I recommend reading the whole of the book before planning your new kitchen and refer back to it at each of the fitting stages. Each chapter is as important as the next as good looking and well-fitted kitchens take time to consider, plan and buy, long before you reach the day for installation.

The chapters, titled 'Fitting Your Own Kitchen' are divided into four manageable sections. They provide a controlled and manageable method of fitting your kitchen, with clear achievable targets to complete before moving on to the next stage. The main section provides instructions for installing textbook kitchens with reasonably straight and square walls. The 'How To' sections show you how to overcome out of square or uneven walls and other problems that may arise, but are not included in the manufacturer's instructions.

TO THE DIY ENTHUSIAST

To become a self-employed independent kitchen fitter requires some 70% knowledge and 30% ability, the combination of this knowledge and ability, added with experience, results in the high level of confidence that is essential when fitting any new kitchen.

A lack of confidence deters many people from attempting to fit their own kitchen, however, once the installation begins, the confidence grows and you can begin to enjoy the sense of achievement as each stage is complete. The aim of this book is to instil the knowledge and confidence you need to fit your own kitchen.

Fitting your own kitchen for the first time can be a daunting prospect when considering the entire project, reading this book and breaking each stage into a number of jobs, will show you that none of them are particularly difficult. Each task requires a fundamental set of skills and a degree of confidence, which, provided you have successfully used basic tools, should be well within your scope.

With the knowledge supplied in this book and the addition of your ability, you should be able to confidently fit your own kitchen to a professional standard and be proud of it for many years to come.

TO THE ASPIRING KITCHEN FITTER

Each section of this book is of equal importance to you if you are planning to become an independent kitchen fitter. Knowledge is 70% of the requirement and if you can prove that you have that, as well as the ability, to a customer that you have only known for five minutes you will probably never be out of work.

Kitchen fitting can be a most rewarding career with job satisfaction second to none. A professional job, image and tools should convey confidence to your customers, which will, in return enhance your reputation as a kitchen fitter around town.

The confidence of a successful kitchen fitter comes from knowing that you have completed a good job once the handles are fitted and the invoice is paid. You will not become 100% confident after completing your first job; it will grow after each job until one day you realise just how good a kitchen fitter you are!

Hopefully this book will have helped you to reach that stage a little quicker than by your own trial and error methods.

Steve Lake - Kitchen Fitter

2 – REPLACE OR IMPROVE?

Deciding whether to replace your kitchen or to improve it, is mainly a question of cost and to some extent, time and disruption. While you may be able to save some money on your kitchen, you will not be able to save on the amount of disruption to your home for at least 3 days, possibly more.

MEASURE FIRST

Most kitchens can be updated but always measure the height and width of each door to make sure replacements are readily available to buy. For doors and drawers of obscure dimensions, there are many companies that will manufacture made to measure doors for you. Tailor made replacement doors may not be the least cost solution but it should still be less expensive than replacing the whole kitchen.

COST SAVINGS

The items typically replaced during a kitchen improvement are; the appliances, sink, taps, doors, handles, drawers, worktops and colour-matched accessories such as end panels and plinths. These items account for 75% of the cost of a new kitchen; therefore it does not mean that you will save half the cost by replacing half the kitchen. Wall and base cupboards account for the other 25% of the cost involved in a new kitchen, they are reasonably priced and obtainable in many sizes from most kitchen suppliers.

You can, of course, choose just to replace the worktops, doors and handles and as long as you choose the style and colour similar to your end panels and other furniture, it will prove the most economical and simple way to update any kitchen.

TIME SAVINGS

The amount of time saved by updating your kitchen, as opposed to installing a complete new one differs for each kitchen. For a new kitchen that would involve five days of fitting, you could aim to save at least two days or more if it all goes to plan. Although updating a kitchen is, in theory, simpler than fitting a complete new one it can still present problems along the way if it is not well planned. If you are replacing colour matched end panels you will probably need to dismantle some wall and base cabinets to refit the panels, worktops may prove difficult to remove depending on how they were fitted. Have a good look at all of the items that you plan to replace and check out how simple or difficult they will be to change before deciding whether to replace or improve your kitchen.

DISRUPTION

Whether you decide to improve or to replace your kitchen, disruption is unavoidable. The only real difference is that if you choose to update your kitchen, the disorder can be managed more effectively than by starting with an empty room.

IN SUMMARY

TO IMPROVE YOUR KITCHEN WILL

- **Save at least 25% of the cost of a new one**
- **Take less time to complete**
- **Involve less disruption to your kitchen**

INSTALLING A COMPLETE NEW KITCHEN WILL

- **Look and feel like a complete, brand new kitchen**
- **Disrupt your daily kitchen routine for approximately 5 days**
- **Last longer than an updated kitchen**

PRICE COMPARISON

Based on replacing worktops, doors, handles, plinth, cornice, pelmets, end panels etc. to a kitchen containing 7 double base cabinets, 7 wall cupboards and a larder unit.

Complete new kitchen (excluding appliances) -	£2,400
Updated (excluding appliances) -	£1,800

My advice: Aim to buy and fit a complete new kitchen within your budget by cutting down on the cost of the doors, accessories and appliances if necessary.

3 – FORWARD THINKING

Thinking and discussion time is a key part to successfully installing a new kitchen. Allow yourself plenty of time to consider the many different tasks to be undertaken. Reading this guide from cover to cover will save you from falling into some of the pitfalls awaiting an unprepared first timer. The more thought and information you have before you start the easier your kitchen will be to install.

CONSIDERING NEW WATER & ELECTRICAL SUPPLIES

Few new kitchens can be installed without some changes to the electrical layout or repositioning of gas, water and waste supplies. If you need electrical or gas work carried out, remember it has to be carried out and certified by professional fitters. You may carry out some minor electrical work but please do check the current regulations first.

Either, obtain a printed plan from your kitchen designer or sketch out your new kitchen layout as early as possible. This will enable you to pinpoint the positions for all new services required.

APPLIANCES

If you are planning to fit built in appliances, you should be aware that space behind them is extremely limited. For washing machines and dishwashers, all pipe work and electrical connections should be fitted into a cupboard next to the appliance. Fitting pipe work at the back will result in the appliance protruding beyond the adjoining cabinets.

The same guide applies to under worktop fridges and freezers. Space is limited behind them and electrical sockets should also be fitted inside an adjacent cupboard.

If pipes must run behind appliances make sure they are fitted close to the wall and as low to the floor as possible. Though it will not guarantee that your appliances fit flush to your cabinets, it will minimise the distance that they protrude.

WALLS AND FLOORS

Examine your existing kitchen to see how it was fitted; this will give you an idea of how easy or difficult it will be when you replace it. Look out for worktops that may have been trimmed or scribed to fit and any modifications to cupboards etc.

Check the conditions of walls and floors. If walls need replastering, patching up or if new floorboards need fitting, make sure it is done before installing your new kitchen.

Notes

4 - PLANNING THE LAYOUT

Now that you have decided to buy a new kitchen and fit it yourself, the next step is to arrange the layout. The advice of a kitchen designer will be of great help at this stage and you can also take advantage of on-line planning tools to design and "view" your kitchen while still in the planning stage.

THE EXISTING KITCHEN

A common method is simply to look at your current kitchen and aim for a direct replacement. My advice is to consider a different view. Picture the kitchen as an empty space, take into account how you have used the kitchen previously and then plan it to be at its most convenient for you and future users. This can be a good way of eliminating annoying areas that you may have had to put up with in your old kitchen.

Following are some common factors to be taken into account when arranging the layout. The main consideration of any new kitchen layout is common sense. The best person to determine the layout is the person that uses the kitchen most often; the next best person is a kitchen designer*.

If you can combine the needs of the main user of the kitchen with the expertise of the designer you will have a kitchen that is not only striking to look at but also practical to use. The following guidelines will help you to determine what is safe and practical and allow you to form a rough layout before the designer arrives. You can then show the designer your layout and they will endeavour to incorporate it into their design and also to ensure that it will fit.

Alternatively, you can measure the kitchen yourself (Chapter 14) and take the measurements to the supplier where they will plan it on their computer for you.

You can use an online planning tool if you prefer to plan the layout yourself. These are available at many kitchen supplier websites. Simply insert the dimensions of your kitchen into the planner and follow the step-by-step instructions until you achieve the look you are seeking. If you are really confident of your measuring and planning, you can even order your complete kitchen on-line! I would advise, however, if it is your first experience of buying a kitchen that you use the human element until you have more experience.

Kitchen designer – Assuming you will be buying the kitchen from one supplier; it is in their interest and yours that they supply the right equipment. At your request, they may arrange for a designer to measure and plan your kitchen free of charge for you. Always check that the service is free beforehand. You are under no obligation to buy, or to have them install the kitchen.

GUIDELINES FOR A NEW LAYOUT

THE KITCHEN TRIANGLE

This is simply a term for the importance of the placement of your three main functional kitchen components - sink, cooker and fridge. This does not mean that you have to place these items as close together as possible; you should, however, aim to place them so that it is convenient to move from one to the other quickly and unhindered.

WASHING MACHINES AND DISHWASHERS

Both appliances are easier placed near the sink, as water and waste fittings are located there. You may place either appliance anywhere in the kitchen but you will need to consider extra plumbing and cabinet modifications when you install the kitchen.

FRIDGES AND FREEZERS

Under worktop fridges and freezers are ideally placed next to each other for convenience of use, unpacking of shopping etc. Tall upright fridge freezers are commonly placed at the end of a worktop where they will not break up useable worktop areas. The same applies to fridge freezers installed into larder units.

OVEN & HOB

There are various options for positioning these appliances; the most convenient is to have the hob set in the worktop with a single or double oven below. This allows easy and direct transfer of hot foods without carrying them across the kitchen. You may opt for an oven to be fitted into a tall cabinet with the hob set in the worktop, bear in mind the transfer of hot food if you consider this option. Freestanding ovens and hobs are another option, while they do not give the kitchen a complete built in look, they are simple to install and simple to replace should you have problems with them. Do not place a hob or cooker directly next to the sink; leave a safe working distance between them of at least 300mm.

DRAWERS

The cutlery drawer should be positioned near to the sink/dishwasher and it is practical to have pan drawers nearer to the cooker. If it were possible to plan a set of drawers in-between the sink and the cooker it would be ideal. If not, it is possible to have a single drawer fitted to a cupboard close to the sink while the pan drawer unit is fitted near the cooker

THE SINK

Always plan to place the sink nearest the water & waste connections, and in front of a window if possible. There is a huge range of sinks available, made from many materials in many sizes. Stainless steel is the easier to maintain and keep looking nice especially if you have a family. For the size of the sink, you will need to take into account the space available below the sink and make sure it will not interfere with other appliances when fitted into the worktop.

WALL AND BASE CUPBOARDS

Plan your kitchen so that each base unit has a wall unit directly above it with the same width doors fitted. This will ensure a designed look to your kitchen with clear straight vertical lines.

Once you have considered this information it is time to get a pencil and paper and sketch out your design. Take rough measurements of the kitchen and keep the sketch as simple as possible, making any notes that you feel are important. Once the kitchen designer arrives you can give them the sketch and notes without the worry of having to remember everything you have discussed.

Notes

5 - SUPPLIERS

There are many competitive suppliers of kitchens in today's market place – most are good honest suppliers but there are, as in every industry, traders to be wary of. I cannot name names in this book so I will leave it to your good judgement to choose a reputable supplier. A visit to any showroom or website will surprise you at the range of kitchens available and the accessories that accompany them.

ASK FIRST

The advice I would offer is to seek advice before deciding on the supplier of your kitchen, ask your neighbours, friends and relatives for their opinions and recommendations concerning their own experiences. Most established suppliers are reasonably reliable as they have many years of experience in the supply business. You may hear some horror stories during your research but do not be put off. Most kitchen nightmare stories are more related to the fitting of the kitchen rather than the supplier. As you will be fitting the kitchen yourself there will be no such stories to retell.

VALUE FOR MONEY

An important point to bear in mind when buying a kitchen, are the appliances, i.e. fridge/freezer/oven etc. While I thoroughly recommend that you buy all of the kitchen cupboards etc from the same supplier, you are not obliged to buy the appliances from them. Sometimes the kitchen supplier will offer a good deal on the appliances and therefore you need look no further. You may however, find that you want to spend less on the appliances or that the supplier cannot supply a particular make/model that you want. As long as the dimensions are the same you can buy appliances from anywhere. Most common appliances are manufactured in only 1 or 2 different sizes; generally in a modern kitchen these will be 600mm wide. You can find appliances measuring 500mm or 550mm, which you may consider designing into your kitchen if space is at a premium.

Take a good look around the showroom before asking the assistant to help you. Have a look inside the cupboards; do they look strong? Does the finish look good? Is the price suspiciously low? Good quality kitchen cupboards are manufactured from either 15 or 18mm thick chipboard faced with melamine. You may find some that are manufactured in 12mm; these will always be less expensive but also less practical. They will look good for a few months but the weight on the shelves begins to show after plates & tins have been on them. If your budget affords it, always aim for the 15 or 18mm cupboards.

DECIDE ON THE WORKTOPS

Worktops are manufactured from many different materials and range in prices from reasonable to extremely expensive. Although this book is based on fitting standard, laminated 40mm thick worktops, you may fit any worktop of your choice. Many suppliers of slate, stone or granite worktops will only supply if they can fit them themselves. As they are highly expensive to buy, fitting is best left to specialists for this type of worktop anyway.

CHOOSE THE DOORS

Once you have decided on the cabinets you will be fitting, the next step is to choose the doors and accessories for your kitchen. This choice I will leave completely up to you – I will only point out that modern faced doors are easier to clean and maintain than natural wood doors, apart from that they all open and close and that is all you need them to do.

HANDLES

The cupboard and drawer handles are a small yet vital part of any kitchen. They need to be stylish enough to make your kitchen look good, yet economical enough to keep your kitchen within budget. An average kitchen will need between fifteen and twenty handles. Prices can range from reasonable to exorbitant per handle. If handles appear unusually expensive from your supplier I would recommend that you shop around for them, as they are available from many outlets.

ARRANGE A VISIT

Once you have decided what you would like, contact the shop or website and ask if they can arrange to visit you at home to measure and plan your new kitchen or you can provide them with your own measured plan. They will then provide you with a simulated picture of how your new kitchen will look, a list of items that you will need to buy and the total cost of it.

DELIVERY TIME

Ask the salesperson regarding the lead-time for delivery of your kitchen. Suppliers can quote anywhere between 2 & 12 weeks to deliver your order. This gives you plenty of time to get any decorating or electrical work completed before the big day.

REFUNDS

Check at the time of ordering whether unwanted items can be returned for a refund. In my experience you will always have extra items that you do not need and if left unpacked, they can be returned for a cash bonus to you at the end.

6 – BUYING YOUR NEW KITCHEN

Your new kitchen will consist of many different components. Choosing them correctly can minimise some of the more difficult tasks when the time arrives for installation. Following is a list of guidelines to consider when selecting your kitchen

FLOOR AND WALL CABINETS

The choice available when buying your new cabinets is between either ready assembled, or flat packed units. Read the following comparison to find the best type for you.

READY ASSEMBLED UNITS

As the description states, these units arrive at your door fully assembled. They are normally fitted with legs, drawers and doors, all you need to do is to fit handles once in position. If you are not seeking to gain the experience, or could do without the hassle of assembling the units, this option could be for you. Obviously the units are more expensive as you are paying for the assembly, they also need a larger storage space when delivered if you are not fitting them on the day of delivery.

FLAT PACKED UNITS

These units arrived in conveniently sized packs and can be stored away until the day of assembly. They are less expensive to buy than ready assembled units, as you will be assembling them yourself. A slight advantage to these units over ready assembled units is that you can modify them, as you assemble them if you need to. You can also leave the back panel loose until the units are fitted in their final positions, which makes it easier if you have holes or shapes to cut away before final fitting.

My choice would always be to buy flat packed units. Once you understand how to assemble the units they will take no more than 15 minutes each to assemble.

As you are going to fit the kitchen yourself, choose base cabinets with adjustable legs on them. These are easier to adjust and make level than cabinets that need shims or spacers fitted to level them. The legs also prevent any ingress of water into the carcass from accidental spills.

Base units with a 50mm gap, or service void at the back are designed to conceal pipes, cables etc in between the back panel and the wall. Most base units are produced with a service gap these days but do check before you buy.

BASE CORNER UNITS

Purpose built corner cabinets are easier to fit as they are supplied as one unit and simply fit into the corner. The second option for a corner unit is to join two standard cupboards into an L shape and fit a corner post to enable doors and drawers to open without interference. Purpose built corner cabinets are slightly more complicated to assemble but easier to fit. Fitting two cupboards together in an L shape with a corner post is easier to assemble but slightly more difficult to fit.

Personally I would choose the purpose built corner cabinet.

WALL CORNER CABINETS

A point to consider when buying wall cabinets is the shape of the unit. This is only to simplify the task of fitting the cornice to the top of the cupboards. Two standard shapes of corner unit available are shown below.

The purpose built corner unit (left) is assembled and fitted to the wall as a one-piece cupboard.

The L shaped corner unit (right) is available either, as a one piece unit, or assembled from two standard units joined together with a corner post.

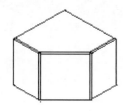
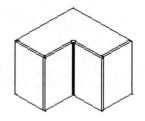

The purpose built shaped cupboard on the left is more difficult to cut the cornice & pelmet for, it has 2 angles of 22.5° as opposed to the unit on the right, which just has one 90° join. For most kitchen fitters the least favourable task is fitting cornice and pelmets to the cupboards. If you are particularly adept with a mitre saw and tape measure the choice is yours, if not choose the L shaped corner unit configuration on the right. If you are not planning to fit cornice or pelmet to your cupboards, it makes no difference which shape you choose.

Choose wall cabinets supplied with adjustable brackets for hanging the cupboard. These are easier to fit and adjust than cupboards that are screwed directly to the wall. The brackets and adjusters allow you to fix the cupboard to the wall and also adjust the height afterwards.

WORKTOP

Standard laminated worktop for use in kitchens is 40mm thick and sold in lengths of between 2 and 4 metres. Before you commit to buy long lengths of worktop, check to make sure that it will physically fit into the kitchen once cut to size. It is rare, but not unheard of, that some kitchens have been fitted, and then walls or doorways have been added at a later date making it impossible to get long lengths of worktop around corners.

There are many different colours, patterns and designs available for laminated worktops but they all have one of three finishes. These are, high gloss, medium gloss or a matt finish.

High gloss worktops are very shiny and reflective, medium gloss is a little less glossy and matt is self-explanatory. High gloss laminated worktops have a tendency to scratch easily and are also more susceptible to show white, burn rings caused by putting hot pans on them.

Medium gloss and matt finish worktop are more durable and easier to maintain than a high gloss finish worktop.

Whichever worktop you choose, read the care and maintenance sheet supplied with it to understand its limitations.

If this will be your first experience of cutting and fitting worktops I would advise choosing a laminated worktop with a medium gloss or matt finish as it is easier to blend in the visibility of the mitred join that you will be cutting.

CORNICE & PELMET

Adding these mouldings to the tops and bottoms to your wall cupboards creates a stylish finish to all kitchens and I would recommend that you incorporate them into your design. They are supplied in a range of different shapes and sizes to match your chosen design.

Unless you have unsightly pipes or cables to hide above the cupboards, aim to buy cornice that is less than 50mm in height. Cornice higher than this is more difficult to cut and fit. If you buy cornice that is above 50mm high you will also need to have, buy or hire a mitre saw with a high cutting area. Most common mitre saws will cope with heights up to 50mm.

SINK & TAPS

I recommend spending as much as you are able on the sink. You will note from your visit to the showroom that the difference in price is huge for what may seem a similar sink. This is mainly due to the thickness of the material of the sink. If you buy a low priced sink you will discover that the taps tend to wobble more so, than on a sink made from a thicker gauge material. Make sure you buy the correct style of tap for the sink. There are 2 types of sink, one has one hole for a mixer or "monbloc" tap, the other has two holes for either 2 single taps or a bar type mixer tap

DRAWERS

Most kitchens suppliers offer 3 types of drawers -

1- Laminated back and sides with a hardboard base and plastic runners

2- Laminated back and sides with a hardboard base and metal runners

3- Steel back and sides with a solid base and metal runners

Option 1 is quite uncommon and should be avoided where possible – they are time consuming to assemble, the drawer bottoms sag after a short time and the runners wear quickly.

Option 2 is a reasonable drawer – the runners last for years but some strengthening will be required to stop the bottom of the drawer from sagging, assembly is tricky too.

Option 3 is the best option, these drawers will last for years with no repairs needed and are simple to assemble (Once you have figured it out!).

Whichever drawers you choose; have a good look at how it is constructed while in the showroom. The knowledge will be useful when the time comes to assemble them for your kitchen.

SOFT CLOSERS

These handy gadgets allow cupboard doors and drawers to close slowly without slamming. These can be fitted to both cupboards and drawers. Although your kitchen supplier will advise you to fit one to every door and drawer, in reality they are not always required, surplus closers can be returned for a refund once the kitchen is complete.

7 – PREPARING FOR THE NEW KITCHEN

There are some preparations that can be made days or weeks before the arrival of your new kitchen and some that can only be made the day (or night) before. Following is a list of preparations and considerations.

Wall and floor tiles can be removed at your convenience anytime before the kitchen arrives. It is best not to remove them too soon as a long time with no flooring or wall tiles can make a kitchen an unhealthy area to work in. It is possible to relay a new floor before the installation of a new kitchen; much care will need to be taken to avoid damage to it during kitchen fitting. I would advise that new floors and wall tiles are always fitted after the kitchen has been installed.

You will have planned any new electrical points* or alterations to the ring main if required. Obviously these will have to fit in with your electrician so you may not have too much control as to when the work is carried out. Do not leave it too late for trade's people to work in your kitchen because if they let you down you will be delayed in starting your kitchen. The same applies to any gas** rerouting that is required. The homeowner can still carry out plumbing, and providing you are not making big alterations, the work will be well within your scope and is explained later in this guide.

*Homeowners may carry out the electrical work but you will need to contact your council to come out and check & certificate any work you have done. If in doubt consult the guidelines at www.partp.co.uk

** Consult a Corgi registered engineer for all gas work.

Make sure you have adequate space to store your old kitchen when it is removed and also your new kitchen when it is delivered. The more space you can make the easier it will be for you at the time of removing and fitting.

Prepare an area to allow the worktop to be stored flat when it arrives, leaning it or allowing it to sag or bend will make the joining process difficult.

It is surprising how much waste packaging you have with a new kitchen. Although most if it can be recycled make preparations for short-term storage.

Important! Telephone your kitchen supplier to confirm that your delivery is loaded or en route before emptying your kitchen.

THE DAY OR NIGHT BEFORE YOUR NEW KITCHEN ARRIVES.

Empty everything from your kitchen except the kettle and tea making facilities, its thirsty work fitting a kitchen! If you own a microwave oven, try to keep it handy for any quick snacks. Arrange the kitchen essentials in a place where you can easily get to them in another room while all non-essential items can be stored out of the way, do bear in mind, your kitchen will be impractical to use for some days to come.

Use the following space to note down jobs that need to be completed before the kitchen arrives

JOBS TO DO BEFORE KITCHEN ARRIVES

8 - FITTING THE NEW KITCHEN

The following 4 stages will guide you from the removal stage up to the final finishing touches for your kitchen. While I advise that you read all chapters before you fit your new kitchen, some stages will become clear only while you are fitting the kitchen. Listed below are some important points to keep in mind while fitting your kitchen.

Wall and base cabinets will only be as straight as the first one – make sure it is level.

Maintain an even overhang of the worktop over the front edge of the cabinets. The overhang should be approximately 40mm along each front edge. Scribe the cabinets or worktop to achieve an even overhang, if necessary. (How To section)

Pay attention to sawing techniques and avoid chipped edges to laminate.

Read instructions supplied with each component at least once

Think and think again before cutting mitres

Keep the working area tidy after each stage of fitting

Respect power tools and their ability to harm you – wear safety equipment at all times

Finally ….

Measure twice, cut once!

Remember – A cheap kitchen can look great if fitted well, equally an expensive kitchen can look cheap if fitted badly. Take your time with each section and have patience.

9 - FITTING THE NEW KITCHEN – STAGE 1

During the first stage of fitting a new kitchen you can expect to dismantle and remove the existing kitchen, mark the walls for your new layout and assemble most of your flat packed cabinets. This stage should take approximately 1 to 1½ days to complete. You will not be fitting doors to the units during this stage as they are fitted during stage 4.

REMOVING THE EXISTING KITCHEN.

The following are guidelines only and are based on the most common fitting methods found in kitchens today. As all kitchens are assembled and fitted in many different ways, you may find that you need to examine the workings of yours further before dismantling or removing.

When you arrive at the sink removal stage with the taps disconnected, fit quarter turn isolating valves to the pipe work to allow the water to be turned back on to the rest of the house. Fit these valves with the arrow on the side pointing in the same direction as the flow of water. Have at least two of these valves to hand before you start disconnecting pipe work.

Similarly, with electricity, make all disconnected supplies safe as soon as possible to allow power to be turned back on for lights/power tools etc.

Kitchens are normally easier to dismantle in reverse order which they were installed. If you propose disposing of your old kitchen you need not be so fussy during the removal process. The following pages explain how to remove the kitchen more or less intact.

DOORS AND DRAWERS

Unscrew the door hinges from the inside of the cupboards and remove doors completely. Pull drawers out as far as they will go, either tilt down and pull, or tilt up and pull. Some older style drawers have a screw on the inside which screws through the side of the drawer and into the runner, if you have this style of drawer, remove the screw and pull the drawer forwards and out. Some drawers are held underneath by plastic lever type clips, move the levers outwards and the drawers should release.

If you are planning to re use the doors or drawers in another area, it is a good idea to mark which cupboards they came from to ease re fitting.

DOORS AND DRAWERS

Remove doors from any built in appliances. Some doors are simply screwed to brackets from the appliance door; others have cleverly concealed fixing devices beneath the seal on the inside of the appliance door and may even be held firm with double-sided tape.

You will need to explore each appliance to discover the way to release it. As you undo each screw, test the door to see if it is becoming loose. Doors that are also held in position with double-sided tape will need to be gently prised off with a wide, flat blade.

WASHING MACHINE & DISHWASHER

Disconnect the electricity supply and tape the power lead to the appliance. Turn off water connections to the appliance at the small quarter turn valves fitted to the pipe work. Disconnect hoses and store inside appliance for future use. Remove waste pipe from its outlet and tape to appliance. If the appliance is built in, remove any screws or brackets holding it in place. Screws into the underside of the worktop hold most appliances in position. Slide the appliance towards you taking care not to damage the legs. Move the appliance out of the kitchen if possible.

FRIDGES AND FREEZERS

Disconnect the electricity supply and hook the cable over the grill at the back of the appliance. If the freezer has an icemaker, disconnect the water supply and turn of at tap. Do not drag either appliance along the floor as this may result in the plastic feet breaking off. If the appliance is built in, remove fixings as above. Move appliances out of the kitchen if possible, don't forget to plug them in again if you have food stored in them!

SINK AND TAPS

Turn off the water to both the hot and cold supply and undo the nuts connecting the pipe work to the taps. Disconnect and remove U bend(s) from the sink unit. Disconnect any earth leads that may be attached to the sink.

At this point you may be able to get access to the clamps, which hold the sink into the worktop. These can be found on the underside of the worktop at the edge of the sink. Loosen the screws with a manual screwdriver until you can move the clamps free of the worktop. If you can access and free all of the clamps the sink should now lift out.

SINK AND TAPS

If not, you may need to gently prise it out, as it should have been sealed to the worktop when installed.

If you cannot get to the clamps at this stage, the sink will have to be removed with the worktop as described in the worktop paragraph later in this section.

OVEN & HOB

If you have a built in oven with the hob set into the worktop you will need to remove the oven first to gain access to the hob. To remove a built under oven, firstly and most importantly, disconnect the power to the oven and remove any fuses fitted to the oven switch on the wall.

If you have a gas oven, turn off and disconnect the gas supply. Depending on the type of connection to your gas oven, you may have to get a corgi registered fitter to disconnect it. If you are not 100% sure of the procedure or if you are not qualified to disconnect gas or electricity supplies, consult a relevant tradesman.

When you are certain that power or gas has been disconnected to both the cooker and hob, proceed as follows; open the oven door(s). On the left and right hand side uprights of the oven, look for either 2 or 4 screw heads that screw through into the cabinet holding the oven in place. Undo and remove the screws and keep in a safe place. You will now be able to slide the oven toward you and down onto the floor. Disconnect any power or gas pipes and cables to the oven and remove it to another room if possible.

To remove the hob – as with the oven, ensure all power and gas is switched off and disconnected before attempting to remove the hob. Look under the hob in the void where the oven was fitted. The hob will either be held in place by screwed clamps or by spring clips. If clamps hold it, undo the screws and remove the clamps, saving them for later use. If the hob is held into the worktop by spring clips the next stage of removal is the same for both types of hob fixings.

Gently press the edges of the underside of the hob to see if it moves slightly, if it does move then continue applying pressure all around the edges until the hob pops out of the cutout. If the hob does not move you may have to gently prise it out, as it should have been sealed in when originally installed. If it does not move at all with gentle prising, look for further hidden screws.

EXTRACTOR FAN UNIT

Disconnect the extractor fan from the electrical supply and remove the fuse from the wall switch if fitted. Remove the mesh cover from the underside of the extractor, which houses the filters and light bulbs. While supporting the unit, remove either, the 4-6 fixing screws that hold the extractor to the wall or check to see if it is held on a bracket. Also check for and remove any screws that may be fixed through the side panel of the extractor into the wall cupboards. Remove the unit.

WORKTOPS

From the underside, remove all screws that appear to be holding the worktop to the cupboards. If you have any corner joints, undo and remove bolts or clamping devices holding the worktop together. Worktops can be held firm by the sealant on the back and side edges, run a sharp knife along these edges to break the seal and loosen the worktop. Lift the worktop upwards; if it moves slightly lift it some more. Repeat lifting the worktop in an up and down motion until it releases itself.

If the worktop does not move once you have removed <u>all</u> of the screws, you may have to cut it away with a saw as it may have been fitted with biscuit joints at the corners. Simply find an area, which is not obstructed by cupboards, cut through the worktop, and lift it out in sections. If the sink clamps were not accessible when you were removing the sink you can simply lift the worktop out with the sink still fitted, and remove the clamps and sink once you have it out.

CORNICE AND PELMET

The cornice is the decorative moulding fitted to the tops of wall cupboards, while the pelmet is the moulding fitted to the bottom edges.

Both these items will be held in place by screws and/or brackets fitted through the top or the bottom of cupboards. Locate and remove the screws, the pelmet & cornice can be simply lifted away. Joints in cornices and pelmets are made with super glue and brackets, to disassemble the joint, remove the brackets and snap the joint apart.

PLINTH

Plinth strips are attached to the legs of cupboards with plastic clips. Their purpose is to cover the gap between the base of the floor cupboards and the floor. To remove them, you should be able to gently pull them off. If the plinth does not seem to be coming off, check for screws through the bottom of cupboards and remove them.

BASE CUPBOARDS

Remove all screws or bolts that are joining the base cupboards together. These may be located behind the hinge brackets. (Already removed) Some or all of the cupboards may be fixed to the wall by a bracket. Remove the screws from the bracket and pull the cupboard forward and out.

Note! Check for any cables or pipes running through cupboards and cut around them with a saw if necessary to remove the cupboard.

SINK CUPBOARD

It is much easier to tidy up any messy plumbing that may have been added over the years and make connections ready for the new sink and appliances while this unit is removed. Leave new water and waste pipes in a position that will make the new sink and appliance connections as simple as possible. Fit quarter turn isolating valves to all open water pipes and turn the water supply back on.

WALL CUPBOARDS

Take out any shelves to make the units lighter when lifting out. Remove all screws or bolts that are joining the cupboards together (behind hinge plates). The cupboards will either be screwed directly to the wall or hung on brackets at each corner. For cupboards screwed directly to the wall, simply remove the screws while supporting the cupboard and withdraw by lifting it towards yourself. Cupboards that are hung on brackets need to be lifted upwards slightly to unhook them, then pulled forwards to remove them. You may need to loosen the two screws in the bracket on the inside of the cupboard at the top if the cupboard will not easily lift up.

LARDER UNITS

Remove screws from brackets holding the larder unit to the wall. Get assistance to lift larder unit to a horizontal position and dismantle the unit on the floor to remove it from the kitchen.

MARKING THE KITCHEN WALLS FOR NEW UNITS.

Place a spirit level along the floor where the cabinets are planned to fit. Find the highest level of the floor and make a mark on the wall at that point. From this mark, measure 870mm* up from the floor and make another mark. This will be your level for the top of the base units. Draw a line from this mark using the level, all the way around the kitchen where the base units are to be fitted. Make a second check that this line is level.

The recommended maximum difference between floor levels is 20mm. If your levels are more than this you will encounter difficulty when fitting the plinths, you will have a higher gap than you have plinth. The problem can either be remedied by levelling the floor prior to installation or by purchasing some long colour matched panels to cut wider plinths from.

You will not be able to mark the line for the wall cupboards yet if you are fitting a larder unit.

If you are not fitting a tall larder/oven unit you can mark a line for the position of the bottom of the wall cupboards at a height that suits you (Fig1) – bear in mind the worktop is 40mm added to your base cabinet line. Once you have marked the line for the bottom of the wall cupboards, measure the height of a wall cupboard and mark the top line of the cupboards. Draw a level line all the way round the kitchen where wall cupboards are to be fitted.

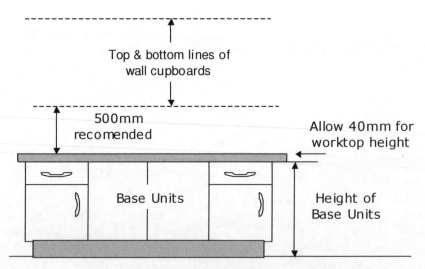

Fig 1 -Setting Height For Wall Cupboards

MARKING THE KITCHEN FOR NEW UNITS.

The lines that you mark on the wall will determine how you fit the cupboards. If the line is not level, you will experience difficulty fitting subsequent cupboards.

Do not mark lines with pen, felt tip or heavy pencil. Cupboards will not cover all lines and they can be hard to decorate over if they are too thick.

* 870mm is a standard dimension. To be sure you are marking the correct height, set a cabinet on the highest point of the floor and to a height that you can fit the plinth under it with a 5 mm gap (Fig 2). Measure the height from the floor to the top of the cabinet; this will be the dimension you need. If you are planning to add new flooring beneath the base units, add the thickness of it to your measurement, i.e. your measurement + 12mm for ceramic tiled floor = 882mm

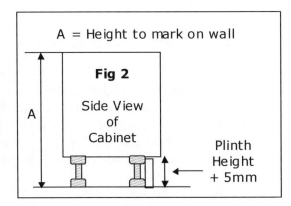

A = Height to mark on wall

Fig 2

Side View of Cabinet

Plinth Height + 5mm

PREPARING TO ASSEMBLE NEW CABINETS.

Before you unpack any units, following are some preparations that will make your experience easier.

Make sure you have a large space in which to assemble the cabinets. Bear in mind, the more cabinets you assemble the smaller this space will become.

Keep your space tidy at all times, dispose of unwanted cardboard/polystyrene etc after each cabinet is installed. This is not only for your safety but also allows you to find the screwdriver that you had just a minute ago!

You will need 3 containers; old biscuit or sweet tins are ideal. These are to store the fittings from each cabinet that you will not be using immediately. One will contain all of the door hinges and plinth clamps, the second will contain left over screws, dowels etc and the third is for the components of the cabinet that you are working on. Using simple systems like this will save you hunting through piles of components while looking for a screw!

TOOLS REQUIRED FOR ASSEMBLING BASE CABINETS

- Hammer – for **gently** tapping nails, fixings and dowels in place
- Large cross-headed screwdriver - manual
- Medium cross-headed screwdriver – manual or battery
- A drill with a 2mm hss pilot drill bit - a battery drill is preferable
- Pliers – for removing dowels placed in wrong holes
- Tape measure

ASSEMBLING THE BASE CABINETS

As your space will be limited, always start by assembling any tall oven/larder units first. Once these are assembled, select the base units in order that they will be fitted, i.e. corner cabinet first, followed by the cabinet next to it and so on. This is because as they are assembled you will stand them in the position that they are to be fitted.

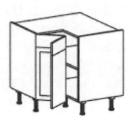

As a rule, all screws and fitting should be visible on the outside of cabinets once assembled. This gives a clean look to the inside. The visible fittings on the outside will be covered by the worktop & plinth.

OPEN THE FIRST CUPBOARD PACK - you will find the following components:

- 1 Solid Base
- 2 Side Panels
- 2 Top Rails
- 1 Back
- 1 Shelf
- 1 Centre support post (only with larger cupboards)
- 1 Pack of fittings
- 1 Instruction sheet

The contents will be the same for most cabinets although a purpose built corner unit will have more components. Some suppliers will include laminated packing pieces in the pack to protect the panels from damage in transit. Only discard these pieces if you are sure that they are packing pieces and not part of the cupboard assembly.

ASSEMBLING THE BASE CABINETS

Take each component and lean it against the wall so you can easily identify them.

Tip the contents of the fittings bag into one of the tins, remove hinges and plinth clips and put them into the 2nd tin and keep for later use. You are now left with the cabinet components and a tin containing screws, dowels and other fittings.

Take the empty cardboard box and tear it along one edge to make a large sheet, lay this on the floor and use it as your protective assembly area.

All cabinets are similar in construction. They consist of a back panel, a solid base panel, 2 solid side panels, a centre post (larger cabinets only) and 2 rails that make the top section. Ensure that when the top rails are assembled, the melamine finish is facing the front of the cupboard. (The back of the cupboard has grooves in it)

Do not fit any hinges or shelf supports at the cabinet assembly stage.

Check whether the side panels of the cupboard you are assembling require colour co-ordinated end panels, if so swap it for the plain one supplied with your cabinet. If you are using full height end support panels instead of co-ordinated end panels, do not fit them at this stage.

TO IDENTIFY AN END PANEL FROM AN END SUPPORT PANEL

A colour co-ordinated end panel is 570mm wide x 720mm tall and is a replica of the plain side panel supplied with your cabinet. It also has pre-drilled holes.

A colour co-ordinated end support is 870mm high and 720mm wide; it has no pre-drilled holes in it.

ASSEMBLING THE BASE CABINETS

Select the two side panels and lay them on the cardboard with the holes facing upwards and the back panel grooves in the centre – Fit dowels and cams to the holes as indicated by the instruction sheet then fit the base, top rails and centre support post to one side panel. Set the other side panel on top and tighten all cams until the cabinet is secure.

Turn the cabinet upside down and fit the feet, use a 2mm drill to make pilot holes for the feet securing screws. Return the cabinet to its upright position and fit the back panel in place. Use 3 of the small nails to hold the back panel on the cabinet but do not hammer them right in, you may need to remove the back panel again for any pipe cut outs. If the back panel for your cabinets makes use of grooves in the cabinet rather than nails to secure it, you will need to fully assemble it at this stage and cut any holes in it while in-situ.

When you have successfully assembled the first cabinet, move it into its position and lay the shelf and instruction sheet inside it, do not fit the shelf at this stage.

Collect the box containing your second cabinet. Tip any leftovers fittings into your third empty tin and begin the process of assembling your second cabinet. Use any cardboard packaging as floor covering as you go.

Repeat the process until you have completed assembly of all of the base units and they are all standing in their planned position.

Cabinets that require a plinth fitted to the sides can either be modified at this stage or while you are fitting the plinth. If you modify the cabinet at this stage you will adjust the position of the legs, if you modify them while fitting you will have to cut a section of the plinth away. This is because when the plinth is fitted to the sides of cabinets, the flange at the top of the leg will prevent the plinth from sitting flush with the side of the cabinet.

With the cabinet upside down, place a plinth clip on each side leg where the plinth is to be fitted. Place a section of plinth in position against the clips and check if the plinth is flush with the side of the cabinet. If the plinth protrudes beyond the cabinet edge, the side legs will need moving in by the same amount.

Modifications are not always necessary, check first before altering the position of the legs.

ASSEMBLING THE BASE CABINETS

THERE IS ONE EXCEPTION to the base cabinet assembly and that is the unit that will contain the sink. When you examine the two top rails of the cabinet you will notice that the gap between them is not wide enough for the sink to sit when fitted. There are 2 options to remedy this, they are:

Option 1 - Modify the cabinet while you build it

To do this you will need to cut the front rail down to approximately 1½" (37mm) wide, and turn the back rail and fit it so that it is vertical rather than horizontal to the cupboard (Fig 2A). This will ensure that when you fit the sink it has plenty of room.

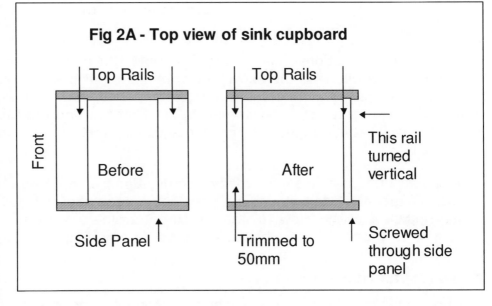

Fig 2A - Top view of sink cupboard

To fit the back rail once it has been changed to vertical, drill and screw through each side of the side panel and into the rail. Set the modified rail at a height that is suitable for the back panel to be fitted once the unit is in place.

When trimming the front rail to size, support it along the length, as it can be easily broken until fitted.

Option 2 - Modify the cabinet when fitting the sink.

To do this you will cut the shape of the sink bowl into the front and back rails of the cabinet with a jigsaw at the time of fitting the sink.

I always choose option one for the sink preparation. Once the worktop is fitted it is difficult to manoeuvre a jigsaw for any cutting that is required. Option 1 also leaves a neater straight edge at the front of the cupboard rather than a crudely cut semi circle.

TALL OVEN OR LARDER UNITS

The same tools and fittings are used for these units but you will need plenty of space and an extra pair of hands, as the units are heavy and cumbersome.

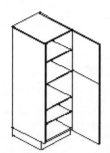

The units normally consist of two packs; one pack containing colour co-ordinated side panels and the other will contain the top & bottom of the unit and the mid section shelves.

ASSEMBLING TALL OVEN OR LARDER UNITS

If your unit is supplied as one pack with plain side panels you will need to discard them for the colour-matched panels if supplied.

Follow the instructions closely and assemble the unit on the floor. When it is complete you will need the extra pair of hands to lift it to its upright position. **Do not** lean it in any way to stand it upright, if you do, you will break the legs. If you and your assistant take one side each, lift if off the floor and turn it while in the air you will get it upright with no damage. **Do not -** drag it into position, lift if carefully.

As these units are used for many combinations of appliances the shelves and back panels are fitted at various positions – read the instructions carefully and see section 4 of the 'How to' chapter to determine the position for each shelf in relation to your particular appliance. Do not fit any hinges at this stage.

PURPOSE BUILT CORNER UNITS

These units can be tricky to assemble depending on the instructions supplied. Follow them carefully and have an extra pairs of hands ready, as they are heavy and easily broken when moved, until fitted. A common assembly fault is fitting panels with the rough face to the front. As with all cabinets it is not a big problem to disassemble it and rectify it.

Now is the time to make sure the units all fit as planned. Stand each unit in its position and take into account any side support panels that are going to be added later.

If they do not fit as planned, you will need to call your friendly supplier for new or different sized cabinets and doors.

If you have to rearrange either the base or wall cabinets for any reason, make sure that above each base cupboard door, there is a wall cupboard door of the same width to maintain the straight lines of the kitchen.

ASSEMBLING THE WALL CUPBOARDS

The routine and tools required for wall cupboards is much the same as for base cabinets. Use the same tins for hinges and leftover fittings; use the cardboard boxes to put on top of the base units for protection. Once you have assembled each cabinet it is safe to store it on top of a base unit temporarily.

Wall cupboard packs consist of

- 2 Side Panels
- Top
- Bottom
- Back Panel
- Pack of Fittings
- Instruction Sheet
- Centre Support (larger cupboards only)

Check each cupboard as you assemble it to determine whether it requires colour co-ordinated end panels. As with the base cabinets, some end panels are direct replacements and some are fitted afterwards. If it is a direct replacement, discard the plain panel(s) supplied with the cupboard and add coloured panel(s).

As a rule, all screws and cabinet fittings should only be visible on the outside of cabinets once assembled. This gives a clean look to the inside. The cornice and pelmets, once fitted, will cover any visible fittings on the outside.

Follow the supplied instructions while assembling cabinets but do not fit any hinges or shelf supports at this stage. When each unit is complete, stand it on a base cabinet in its corresponding position. Place the shelf and the cupboard hanging brackets inside the cupboard along with the instructions.

10 - FITTING THE NEW KITCHEN – STAGE 2

The second stage of fitting your kitchen will see the base cabinets secured, the wall cupboards and extractor unit fixed to the wall and the drawers assembled and fitted. Stage two will again take between 1 and 1½ days to complete.

IF YOUR KITCHEN CONTAINS A TALL OVEN/LARDER UNIT

Before you can mark the wall for the height of the wall cupboards, you must first set the tall larder unit in its final position as the top of this unit defines the line for the top of the wall cupboards. (Fig 3)

To ensure the larder unit is in its final position you must first fit and level some of the base units. You will screw the base units to the wall at this stage, but you may need to remove them again when fitting the wall cupboards.

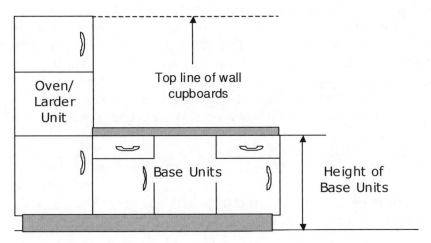

Setting Height For Wall Cupboards - Fig 3

TOOLS REQUIRED

- Spirit levels – one 600mm long and one a minimum of 1000mm long are ideal
- Power Drill & drill bits – Masonry 10 or 12 gauge + 4mm high speed wood bit
- Extension lead
- Selection of screwdrivers
- Cable detector
- Cordless Screwdriver
- Handsaw

TOOLS REQUIRED

- Tape measure
- Safety Equipment
- 2 soft-faced clamps
- Jigsaw with fine-toothed blade
- Pencil

Remove the wall cupboards from their overnight position on top of the base units and stand them away from the fitting area.

While fitting base units you may need to cut sections from the service area of the side panels or areas of the back panels to allow for pipes, cables or skirting boards. Only mark and cut these areas once the height of the unit has been established. Use a fine-toothed jigsaw or hole saws for any cutting required and avoid cutting areas that contain metal fittings. Make sure cut outs are large enough to allow appliance connections and power plugs to be easily accessed.

Move the first corner unit into its position and ensure that it sits squarely into the corner. Adjust the legs to level the unit to the lines marked on the wall previously. An assistant will be invaluable here for this.

Lie on the floor so that you have access to each of the adjustable legs. Turn the legs by hand to either raise or lower the unit to the desired level. First adjust the back legs so the top of the cupboard is in line with the line drawn on the wall. Next, adjust the front legs so that the cupboard is level to the spirit level. You may have to go back to each leg 2 or 3 times to ensure the cupboard is in line with your drawn line, level at the front and standing at 90° to the floor. The first cupboard is the hardest to level, once this one is set the remainder of the cupboards are much easier.

Check now to see how the plinth will fit – measure the gap below the cupboard where the plinth attaches to the legs. The distance from the floor to the underside of the cupboard should be approximately 5mm greater than the width of the plinth. If it is much more or much less you will need to recheck the wall marking made earlier.

Once the corner unit is level, fit 2 small brackets to the sides of the cupboard, at the top on the inside and secure to the wall.

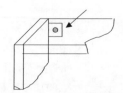

Make sure you nail the back panels on fully, before securing to the wall and once any alterations have been made!

END PANELS

The purpose of an end support panel is almost self-explanatory. It is a panel that fits on an end and supports the worktop. They can be fitted either side of an appliance or cabinet to give a decorative finish rather than being able to see the plain white of a cabinet. The third use that is not explained by the description is the "boxed" in effect they give. You will notice that when you fit a support panel, the bottom of it sits forward of the plinth area, it is when the plinth is fitted that it gains its "boxed" in look Do not be tempted to cut the front of the panel to suit the plinth, if you do not like the appearance of the "boxed" look you can change it once the kitchen is fitted.

Fit end support panels as you go if they are required. Hold a panel against the side of the cupboard with the bottom edge on the floor with an equal space along the front edge of the cupboard. If the panel is taller than the cupboard, mark a pencil line along the top edge. Saw the panel along this line with a handsaw, (jigsaws do not cut perfectly straight lines.)

When the panel is the correct size, clamp it to the side of the cupboard and decide how you will fix it. You can either drill 4 pilot holes through the inside of the cupboard, or, use 4 holes on the inside of the cupboard that are pre-drilled for shelf support studs. If you choose the latter you will need to ensure they are not in a position that you might put a shelf.

Select 4 screws that will secure the panel and screw through the cupboard **into** the end panel. Make sure the screws **are not** long enough to go right through the cupboard <u>and</u> end panel!

Put the next cupboard to be fitted in position against the corner unit. Starting at the legs nearest to the corner unit, adjust them up or down so that the top and bottom of the unit are flush with the top and bottom of the corner unit. Adjust the other legs so that the unit is level in all directions. Once level, attach brackets and secure to wall.

Leave gaps between the cupboards for any fitted appliances. Check with the supplied instructions to determine the gap required for your particular appliance. These will be fitted into position later.

Do not join the cabinets together at this stage; you may need to remove them individually to fit the wall cupboards. Continue levelling units and securing to the wall until you arrive at the larder unit.

OVEN/LARDER UNIT

You will need assistance to steady the tall larder unit while you are levelling it.

Place the larder unit against the side of the last base unit. Adjust the legs of the larder unit nearest to the base unit until the bottom of the larder is flush with the bottom of the base unit. Adjust the legs on the other side of the larder unit until it is standing at 90°. Do not raise or lower one side of the larder unit too much at once, it will cause it to tilt and become unstable.

When the larder unit is level and straight in all directions, secure it to the wall using a minimum of 4 small L brackets.

You now have the position for the top line of the wall cupboards. Place a spirit level on top of the larder unit and draw a level line on the walls in the position that the wall cupboards are to be fitted.

You are now ready to fit the wall cupboards. Again, an assistant will make the task much easier.

You may find it easier to unscrew and remove any base cabinets that are in your way while hanging wall units. Make sure you replace them in exactly the same position.

CUPBOARD END PANELS – if you have the type of colour matched end panels that screw onto the side of the cupboard rather than being a part of the cupboard, note the following.

The panels should not require cutting to size. They may seem to be wider than you would expect but there is a reason for it. When these panels are screwed to the side of a cupboard, they protrude along the front edge. When the door is fitted it gives a "boxed in" effect. Simply screw these panels, (from the inside of the cupboard) where required, to the sides of cupboards that need them, normally at the end of a run of cupboards or either side of the extractor.

Start by fitting the first corner wall cupboard. Follow the instructions supplied with the unit for hanging the cupboard. The corner cupboard is critical to get level as it affects all other wall cupboards.

HANGING WALL CUPBOARDS

Measure and mark positions for the hanging brackets and secure to the wall using suitable fixings for your type of wall. To mark out the wall bracket positions, hold a bracket under the wall unit hanger. Measure from the top of the unit to the centre of the fixing holes in the wall bracket. Transfer measurement (A) to the wall, measuring down from the line that represents the top of the wall units. Measure the width of the wall unit and draw a vertical line to indicate the side edge of the wall unit

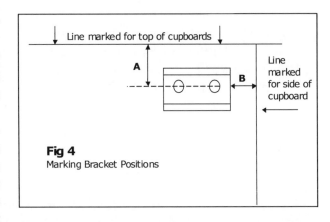

Fig 4
Marking Bracket Positions

once fitted. Make a mark 20mm (B)* in from this line and that will be the position for the edge of the wall bracket.

*Dimension B may be reduced, depending on the thickness of your cupboards

Use a cable detector to ensure there are no pipes or cables in the position you are drilling. When drilling the holes for the brackets, angle the drill slightly downward, this will give a stronger fixing and prevent the screws working loose.

Lift the corner unit into position and ensure the hooks of the cabinet hang on the brackets. When you are sure all is engaged, as it should, it is safe to let go. Place a spirit level on top of the cabinet to check it is straight. If it needs adjustment, you will find two adjusting screws in the cupboard bracket (Fig 5). One screw will raise or lower the cabinet and the other is used for pulling the cabinet tight to the wall.

Once you have established that the line for the brackets is correct you can then extend the line all to all areas requiring wall cabinets using a spirit level and pencil

If your cabinets have a solid back and do not have adjustable hanging brackets, a different fixing method is required. For these units, fix a straight batten to the wall level with the line for the bottom of the cupboards. Mark and drill a 5mm hole in each corner of back of the wall cupboard. Place the cupboard onto the batten and mark the positions for the holes through the cabinet back. Remove the cupboard and drill and plug the holes. Replace the unit to its position and fix with screws.

Check with your instructions as to which screw adjusts the unit up or down and adjust to suit. (Fig 5) If your cabinet also requires screws through the back mid section to support it, mark these holes now. Take the cabinet down and drill & plug the holes for these screws. Re hang the cabinet, when the cabinet is level in all directions, tighten the screws that pull the cabinet tight to the wall and screw the fixings through the mid section holes.

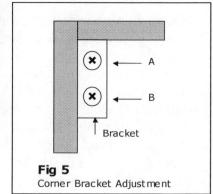

Fig 5
Corner Bracket Adjustment

Follow the same procedure of marking bracket positions and securing the brackets to fit the next cabinet. Hang the cupboard on the brackets and repeat any height adjustments as for the corner unit. Make sure the tops and bottoms of both cabinets are flush with each other. Tighten the screws that pull the cabinet tight to the wall, as required. The two cabinets can now be joined together

There are 2 methods for joining cabinets, one is to use two-piece joiners, and the other is to use plain screws. If you were supplied with, and intend using two-piece joiners, drill two 5mm holes through the sides of the cupboards to be joined, and fix together.

If you are using screws, drill two pilot holes through the side of one cupboard. The ideal position for either two-piece joiners or screws is behind the hinge plate. Determine which 2 pre-drilled holes the hinge will fit to (normally 2nd & 3rd from top and bottom) drill between these holes and screw or bolt the cabinets together. The hinge, if fitted, will hide the screw head or bolt. If you are joining cupboards on the non-hinged side of the cupboard, the head of the bolt or screw will be visible but may be covered with a plastic cap.

Continue fitting wall cupboards and joining them together until you reach the tall larder unit. Joining a cupboard to a larder unit is the same as joining cupboard to cupboard. The top of the wall cupboard should be flush with the top of the larder unit.

When you reach the extractor fan unit, either fit the short cupboard if you have an integral extractor or leave a gap the exact width of the extractor (normally 600mm) and return fit it once all of the wall cupboards are hung.

If you have another corner cabinet or larder unit, repeat the above steps until all of the cupboards are fitted and secure.

FITTING DECORATIVE UNITS

Some units such a wine racks and open cupboards do not have hanging brackets as a means of fixing. This is because doors are not fitted to the unit and any fittings would be visible.

Hang all of your standard wall cupboards and leave a gap the exact size of any decorative units. Position the open unit in the gap and hold in position with clamps. The unit can now be joined to the other cupboards using screws or two-piece joiners.

A tip to make positioning of these units easier is to temporarily screw a batten across the top centre of the unit, overhanging the sides by 200mm. The unit can then simply be hung in place with the batten providing support, giving you freedom to secure the clamps.

Screw through adjoining cupboards into the decorative unit, this method will leave no screw heads visible on the decorative unit. Added support can be given by fitting angled brackets at the top between the unit and the wall.

For open-end wall corner units, the batten method cannot be used and clamps will be required to hold it in position while joining. These units also require securing by drilling and screwing through them into the wall. Cover any exposed screws with plastic screw caps.

SECURING THE BASE UNITS.

Once the wall cupboards are all fitted and secure, install the remainder of the base cabinets around the room and join them together using the two-piece joiners or screw method described above. Check it all again to ensure it is still level. Check to make sure all feet are touching the floor and adjust them downward if necessary.

The base units should all feel solid once screwed to the walls and bolted together. You should not be able to feel any movement if you give them a gentle shake. Once the worktop is fitted it will give extra stability to all of the units.

FITTING THE EXTRACTOR FAN UNIT

As there are so many types and models of extractor in circulation today, it is impossible to provide detailed instructions as to how to fit them. As a guide, the following are points common to most of them.

Most are fitted to the wall by either screws or brackets at the back of the extractor. A template for marking screw positions is normally supplied with the extractor.

For extra support some are screwed through the side into wall cabinets.

FITTING THE EXTRACTOR FAN UNIT

There is a minimum height at which to fit an extractor above a hob, normally 600mm for electric and 750mm for gas – check your installation guide first.

To access the screws/brackets, remove the mesh covers from the underside of the unit.

Refer to instructions regarding the modes in which the extractor functions.

TO ASSEMBLE THE DRAWERS AND FIT THE RUNNERS TO THE CABINETS

Although the assembly and quality of drawers has improved immensely over the years, drawer fitting can be a frustrating item to attempt. My advice is to have patience, if you find you are struggling with them, take a break, do a different job and return to them later. Once you have assembled one you will see how simple they are.

As with extractor units, today's range of drawers and runners is vast and beyond any direct help here for your particular set. The following is based on common drawers and runners and hopefully will be of use to you.

A drawer pack consists of:

• 2 sides – one left and one right
• 1 back
• 1 base
• 1 drawer front
• 1 pack of fittings

DRAWERS

Do not fit any handle to any drawer until you know you have correctly assembled and fitted them.

Only open 1 pack at a time. Identify each component so that you know what it is. Read the assembly instructions carefully as not all of them are very clear.

Most of the metal drawer frames clip together by some means at the back, the base is then fitted and secured with 2 or 4 screws to hold it all together.

DRAWERS

A fitting is screwed to the inside of the drawer front that enables you to clip the drawer onto the drawer front.

DRAWER RUNNERS

There are 2 runners to each drawer. One will be marked left, the other right.

Follow the diagrams supplied with the runners and fit them onto the cabinet by means of the predrilled holes and screws.

Fitting and adjusting drawers

Put the drawer on its runner and push it into the cupboard. If you have the latest metal slow closing drawers you will hear a click as they engage themselves. If you have laminated drawers you may need to connect the drawer to the runner with a screw through the side panel of the drawer into the runner.

When you push the drawer fully in, the top of the top drawer should be level or just below the top rail of the base cabinet. If it is out by a few millimetres you can adjust it, if it is out by more than 6mm you may have the drawer front upside down. Remove the drawer front and replace it the other way up.

To remove drawers once engaged, look underneath the drawers for two plastic clips and move these towards the centre and pull the drawers out.

When you have the top drawer finished and fitted, repeat the steps for the other drawers. Consult your instructions for methods of adjustment. Normally there are 2 screws at either side of the front of the drawer. One will adjust the drawer up and down; the other adjusts it left to right or vice versa.

Make sure all drawers slide in and out easily and that all screw heads are firmly tightened and not rubbing on the drawers.

11 - FITTING THE NEW KITCHEN – STAGE 3

On successful completion of this fitting stage you will have cut and fitted the worktops, fitted and plumbed the sink and have the hob set into the worktop waiting connection.

WORKTOPS

This section explains how to fit worktops with mitred joints cut with a router using a jig for guidance. If you have chosen to use joining strips to make corner joints instead, please refer to section 1 of the 'How To' section at the back of this guide for further instructions.

Whichever your chosen method, make sure that you have read and understand the instructions and health and safety guides supplied with power tools. If this is your first time using a router, practice first to understand its capabilities and manoeuvrability controls.

The following procedure is for worktops fitted in a U shape, it consists of 2 corner joints, a cut out for the sink and another for the hob. It is assumed that the corners of the kitchen where worktop is to be fitted are square. For out of square corners follow the guidelines in the 'How To' section at the end of this book

PREPARATION

Worktops are heavy! Arrange to have an assistant with you for this stage. You will also need an area large enough to accommodate the workbenches and worktop as well as space for you to be able to use the router while cutting the worktop.

Handling worktop carefully is of the utmost importance. If it is knocked against doors or furniture it will chip. There are some products that will disguise small chips and dents but the best way is to handle with extreme care at all times. This is particularly important when butting two mitred joins together. Always slide the joints gently together where possible and if you have to drop one joint into the other, use a sheet or two of newspaper to protect the cut edge.

TOOLS REQUIRED FOR CUTTING AND FITTING THE WORKTOP

Router fitted with 30mm collect and 12.7mm cutter

Worktop Jig & Instructions	Tape Measure & Pencil
4 soft-faced clamps	10mm Spanner
Extension Lead	Fixing Bolts – 3 per joint
Jigsaw	Worktop Sealant – close colour match
Masking Tape	File
Combination Square	PVA or Varnish
Contact Adhesive	3 Workbenches

The diagram below shows the preferred worktop configuration for U shaped kitchens. The instructions following will refer to this diagram.

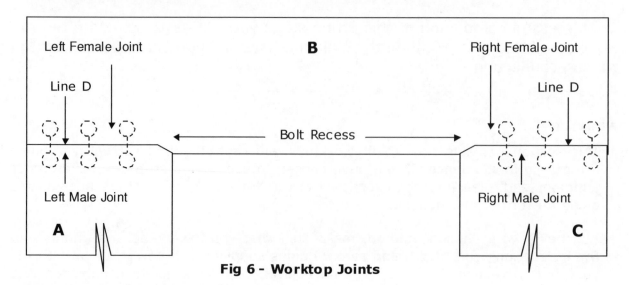

Fig 6 - Worktop Joints

ORDER OF FITTING WORKTOP

Measure & cut Section B to length

Cut female joints and bolt recesses to section B.

Measure & cut Section A, 75mm oversize and cut male joint with bolt recesses

Measure & cut Section C, 75mm oversize and cut male joint with bolt recesses

Trim Sections A & C to length

Mark and cut holes for sink and hob

Join worktop joints with bolts and joint sealer.

When fitting worktops it is easier to cut them longer and trim them to size later if possible. If you have a tall oven/larder unit at the end of the worktop it will make fitting simpler if this is temporarily moved to allow for an over cut of the worktop. If you are cutting to fit against a larder unit or return wall, see section 2 of the 'How To' guide.

Only cut from left to right with the router at depths of 15mm per cut. Only cut into the rounded edge of the worktop. Cutting against the direction of the router will damage the blade and chip the worktop.

MEASURE AND CUT SECTION B TO LENGTH

Measure the length of worktop required for section B and deduct 4mm, this will allow a 2mm fitting gap on sides A & C. Apply masking tape to the area of the worktop to be cut and mark the cutting lines in pencil.

Place the worktop on the workbenches and hold secure with clamps. Cut along the lines with a saw or jigsaw ensuring that the whole of the worktop is supported on workbenches.

Once cut, lay the worktop in position to make certain it fits.

If clean straight edges are required for section B, refer to section 3 of the 'How To' guide and cut the edges with a router.

TO CUT THE LEFT HAND FEMALE JOINT – SECTION B

Position the worktop face down on the workbenches with the rounded edge nearest to you. Although you will be cutting the join on the right hand side of the worktop, into the rounded edge, this will be the left hand side once the worktop is face up.

Set the jig in the position indicated by the instructions to cut a left hand female joint. Make sure 2 locating pegs are positioned in the holes marked "F" and the other 2 are in the correct holes indicated for the width of your worktop.

Place the jig, with all pegs firmly against the rounded edge and side of the worktop and ensure it is square. Once the jig is in its position, secure it to the worktop with soft faced clamps. Clamp the worktop to the workbenches with another 2 clamps and check to make sure all is secure before cutting.

Check the cutting slot of the jig is parallel to the rounded edge. Measure from the back of the cutting slot to the back of the worktop, this measurement should be exactly the same at either end of the jig. Adjust if necessary. If all locating pegs are in contact with the worktop, no adjustment should be necessary.

Position the router in the extreme left corner of the cutting slot, set the cutting depth to 15mm and start the router. Pass the router along the slot, using the edge nearest you to guide the router. Repeat the process, increasing the cutting depth by 15mm each time until all of the waste has been removed.

Set the cutter to maximum depth and pass the router along the slot again using the side furthest from you to guide the router. This final pass will remove approximately 1mm, leaving a perfectly cut edge.

BOLT RECESSES

With the worktop face down on the worktables, place pegs in holes marked B and set the jig to the position indicated by the instructions for cutting bolt recesses.

Clamp the jig to the worktop and set the router cutter to approximately 20mm. Starting with the mushroom shaped recess on the left, guide the router clockwise around the slot removing all of the waste. Repeat the process for the other 2 slots.

Turn the jig over and repeat the process for the opposite bolt recesses. Place a bolt in the recess to ensure that it sits flush or just below the surface of the worktop.

TO CUT THE RIGHT HAND FEMALE JOINT – SECTION B

Repeat the cut for the left hand female joint but set the worktop face upwards.

You will now have a length of worktop with both female joints and bolt recesses cut. This is Section B of the worktop almost ready.

MEASURE AND CUT SECTIONS A & C TO LENGTH

Measure the distance from line D (cut edge) to the end of your worktop run, add 75mm to the length and cut the worktop squarely.

If you have a larder unit or return wall at the end of the run of cupboards see Section 2 of the How To section, this will show you how to cut it to length.

TO CUT THE LEFT HAND MALE JOINT – SECTION A

Position the worktop face up on the workbenches. Set the jig in the position indicated by the instructions to cut a left hand male joint. Make sure 2 locating pegs are positioned in the holes marked M and are flush with the rounded edge of the worktop.

Place the combination square along the flat, back edge of the worktop and check that the jig is set square. Clamp the jig to the worktop and the worktop to the workbenches.

TO CUT THE LEFT HAND MALE JOINT – SECTION A

Position the router in the extreme left corner of the cutting slot, set the cutting depth to 15mm and start the router. Pass the router along the slot using the edge nearest to you to guide the router. Repeat the process, increasing the cutting depth by 15mm each time until all of the waste has been removed.

Set the cutter to maximum depth and pass the router along the slot again using the side furthest from you to guide the router. This final pass will remove approximately 1mm, leaving a perfectly cut edge.

BOLT RECESSES

Follow the same process for cutting bolt recesses as described for section B of the worktop.

Measure the centres of the bolt recesses in Section B and check they will match up before cutting.

Starting with the mushroom shaped recess on the left, guide the router clockwise around the slot removing all the waste. Repeat the process for the other 2 slots.

TO CUT THE RIGHT HAND MALE JOINT – SECTION C

Repeat the above process to produce the right hand male joint but set the worktop face down on the workbench. To cut the bolt recesses for the right hand male joint, repeat the process for section A, but with the jig turned the other way up.

TRIM SECTIONS A & C TO LENGTH

Place section A into position, butted up to, but not bolted to Section B. Check that the joints line up and the bolt recesses are aligned correctly. Draw a pencil line on the underside of the worktop flush with the top of the end of the run of cupboards; this will give the finished length of the worktop. If you prefer the worktop to overhang the cupboard, add the overhang dimension to the marked line before cutting. Cut this line with a saw, or if using a router for a perfect straight cut; see part 3 of the 'How To' section.

For section C, repeat the process as for Section A

ADJUSTING THE ANGLE OF THE JIG

The jig may be adjusted to cut joints of more or less than 90°. However, unless you are very experienced at using the jig I would not recommend attempting to do so. Ensuring the worktop is square by scribing it is the simplest way for a beginner to fit worktops.

MARKING AND CUTTING THE HOLE FOR THE SINK

Place the sink upside down in the desired position on the worktop. Make sure the sink is positioned central to the cupboard below and that there are will be no obstructions once the sink is set in the worktop. Mark a line around the outside of the sink with a pencil. If the worktop is too dark for a pencil line to be visible, apply masking tape to the areas to be marked.

Remove the sink from the worktop and mark another line, 10mm* in from the sink outline. This will be the line to cut for the sink to sit in.

Remove the worktop and place it across 2 workbenches for ease of cutting. Drill a 10mm hole just inside the cutting line at each corner. Cut round the lines with a jigsaw ensuring the waste section is supported on the final cut. Once cut, check the sink will sit in the hole with the edges of the sink flush on the worktop. Seal all cut edges with PVA to provide a waterproof protection.

*Check measurements with supplied instructions before cutting.

MARKING AND CUTTING THE HOLE FOR THE HOB

Read the installation instructions supplied with the hob and obtain the dimensions for the size of the hole to be cut for the hob. Place the hob on the worktop and ensure it is central to the extractor unit and the cupboard below Repeat the process for marking and cutting the sink cut out. Make sure the position of the marked hole is square and parallel to the front edge of the worktop.

JOIN WORKTOP JOINTS WITH BOLTS AND JOINT SEALER

Place sections A & B of the worktop in position and ensure that the bolts will be accessible from the underside once joined. (You may have to cut away an area of the top rail of the cupboard to do this.) Apply a bead of joint sealer to one cut edge of the worktop by raising the joint at an angle, lower the joint and wipe away any excess sealer forced out. Worktop sealer is available in colour-matched tubes for sealing worktops. If using silicone as a sealer, apply an extremely thin film to one face only, too much will cause the joint to swell.

From the underneath of the worktop, fit the three joining bolts and tighten each one a little at a time, checking the joined worktops are flush along the length of the joint. Once the joint is almost tight, remove excess sealer and very gently tap the worktop flush with a hammer using a scrap piece of wood as protection before fully tightening the bolts.

Be extremely careful when joining, tightening and tapping worktop, as the laminate edges are brittle until fully joined and sealed.

ATTACHING PROTECTIVE END COVERINGS.

ALUMINIUM END CAPS are my preferred choice to protect worktop ends from damage; these are available in a range of finishes to suit your kitchen. They are simply cut to size and screwed into the sawn edge of the worktop. A lip on the end cap sits over the cut edge of the worktop to protect it from bumps and knocks. While laminate strips can look smarter at the end of worktops, aluminium end caps will not chip and will protect the edge for life.

LAMINATE STRIP supplied with the worktop can also be fitted but offers less protection to exposed ends. To fit the laminate ends, cut the laminate to the approximate shape of the worktop end. Apply impact adhesive to both the laminate strip and the worktop end; allow them to become touch dry before applying the laminate to the worktop edge.

Once dry, using a file at a slight upward angle; remove excess laminate until you achieve a flush finish. The underside edge will have a greater overhang and this also needs removing with a file until flush.

FITTING THE SINK

Lay the sink upside down on cardboard for protection. Fit the retaining clips to the underside of the sink to the instructions supplied with the sink. Ensure the clips are spaced evenly around the sink and that the gripping edges of the clips are facing away from the sink.

Apply the sealing strip, supplied with the sink, to the top edge of the sink cut out. Peel back the protective film and stick the strip in one continuous piece, avoiding wrinkles at corners. Trim the sealing strip at the join ensuring no overlap.

Offer the sink into position, checking for any obstructions from the cabinet below. You may need to cut an area of the top rails away if you have not already done so. Once the sink is in position and sitting flush all the way round, check that you can access all of the securing clips. Remove the sink and chisel or cut away any areas of the cabinet that will prevent the clips being fitted correctly.

From the underside of the sink, tighten each clip in turn until it just bites the worktop. Tighten the clips further, in sequence, front, and back, left and right, until all clips are tight and the sink is flush on all sides with the worktop.

FITTING THE HOB

Fit the foam sealing strips or putty like material to the top edge of the cut out and check for obstructions in the same manner as for fitting the sink. Place the hob in position making sure it sits flush to the worktop on all faces. Secure from the underside using the clips or clamps supplied with your hob unit. If the hob requires a gas supply, make certain that there is sufficient access for the connection.

SECURING THE WORKTOP

To secure the worktop to the cupboards, drill one pilot hole through each of the top rails of the base cupboards and screw through into the worktop. Alternatively, screw through brackets supplied with the cabinet and into the worktop.

SECURING END SUPPORT PANELS

If you are using end support panels in the mid section of the worktop, fix these to the worktop and floor, using L shaped brackets. Position the brackets, two at the top and two at the bottom, away from the front of the worktop and out of sight. Make sure the brackets will not interfere with the feet of any appliance that will be fitted later.

FITTING SPLASH BACKS

Splash backs are cut to size with mitred corners and generally fixed to the wall using a no-more-nails type adhesive. Apply sealant to the top and bottom edges for a waterproof fit. These are best fitted once any tiling is complete.

PLUMBING THE SINK

If you have not yet prepared the plumbing connections, see part 5 of the 'How To' section for a basic kitchen configuration.

If your taps are supplied with solid connecter pipes you may find it easier to dispose of them and replace with flexible braided tap connector hoses.

Attach the flexible braided hoses to the tap and pass through the hole in the sink. Fit the tap to the sink following the instructions supplied with it. Ensure that the nut holding the tap in position is tightly secured to prevent any movement from the tap. Connect the flexible hoses to the previously prepared water supply pipes.

Fit the waste and overflow fittings to the sink, applying hand pressure only to tighten plastic nuts. Connect your chosen style of U bend to the waste fitting of the sink. Using a combination of 40mm pipe and angled or straight connectors, join the U bend outlet to the previously prepared waste pipe outlet. Only apply adhesive to the fittings once you have them configured correctly.

TESTING THE PLUMBING

With the sink taps in the off position, open the quarter turn valve to the cold supply slightly and check and rectify any leaks before opening the valve fully. With the plug fitted to the sink, turn the cold tap on, and again check and rectify any leaks. Repeat the process for the hot water supply until you have water to both hot and cold taps, with no leaks.

If you have appliance inlets on the U bend connector, make sure these are temporarily sealed. Lift the plug from the sink to allow a small amount of water through the waste system and check and rectify leaks. Turn the taps to medium flow and allow the water to run through the waste systems for a few minutes, checking and rectifying any leaks at the same time. Replace the plug in the sink and allow the sink to fill to the overflow level and check that for leaks. Leave the water in the sink for 30 minutes to ensure it does not leak between the waste connector and the sink. Finally pull the plug out and allow the water to escape at full speed through the waste system.

Make a final check of everything you have installed so far. Check all cabinet legs are adjusted down, all screws are tightened up and the worktop is secure at each section.

You have now completed stage 3 of fitting your kitchen!

12 - FITTING THE NEW KITCHEN – STAGE 4

This stage will see the end of your project. You will fit the cornice, pelmet and plinths, install and connect all appliances and fit all shelves, doors, drawers and handles.

SHELVES

Fit the shelves to cupboards before you fit the doors, as it is easier to manoeuvre them without hinges in the way. Simply press two shelf support studs into the predrilled holes on each side of the cupboards and one into the centre support pillar (if fitted). Shelf height can easily be adjusted at a later date by moving the support pegs to other holes.

The shelf for the cupboard containing the sink will require cutting if the U bend is in the way. Hold the shelf in position just below the obstruction and mark an area to be removed large enough to clear the obstruction, then cut with a jigsaw.

DOORS AND HINGES

Select a base unit door and screw the hinges to it following the instructions supplied. Decide which way the door should open, and then hold the door against a cupboard to determine which holes are for the hinge plate. Fit the hinge plate to the cupboard and attach the door, either by clipping it on or by means of a securing screw. Repeat the process until all doors are fitted. Once all doors are fitted they can be adjusted by means of adjusting screws in the hinges, as diagram. Use a door as a test to see how the door moves once the adjustment screws are turned.

As you face the cupboard, adjust the screws using the diagram and notes below

A   Slacken of both screws to adjust the cupboard door either upward or downward

B   Loosening will enable you to adjust the gap between the door and the cupboard **(D).** This gap is often the reason that doors will not close flush with the face of the cupboard.

 The gap **(D)** should be even along the length of the door.

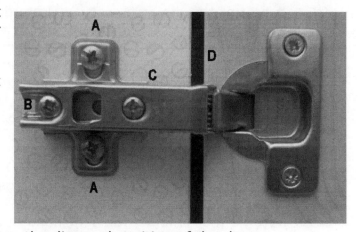

C   Adjust this screw, in or out, to change the diagonal position of the door.

DOORS AND HINGES

Nicely fitted doors are essential for a professional finish to your kitchen. Adjust each screw on the first door to understand the affect is has before adjusting the rest of the doors.

Doors are slightly smaller than the cupboards, this is to allow a small gap between each door to enable it to open and close without rubbing against the door next to it.

Appliance doors are either simple to fit, or extremely frustrating. As there are so many combinations of fitting methods used for these doors it is impossible to give any advice further than to follow the supplied instructions very carefully and have patience!

FITTING HANDLES

Another "small" job that is critical to the finish of the kitchen is to fit the handles in a straight and uniform manner. The job can be made quite simple by making up a template (Fig 8), from stiff cardboard, to mark out the position of the holes before drilling.

Wall cupboards - First, decide on the position of the handles for the doors, and then mark the positions (A) for the required holes lightly onto the back face of one of the left hand doors. Place the template (B) squarely into the corner as shown in the diagram below and transfer the positions of the holes onto the template, drill through the template and write "left" on the face of it, this will now be used for all left hand wall cupboard doors. Turn the template over and mark "right" on it; this will be used for all right hand wall cupboard doors.

With the template flush with the corner edges of the inside of the left hand door, mark the position of the holes with a pencil. Hold a piece of scrap wood firmly to the front face of the door and drill a 2mm hole through each mark. From the front face of the door, enlarge the holes using a 4mm drill. This way of drilling will reduce any chipping to the doors when the drill bit breaks through the face. Screw the handle into position and check that it is straight before drilling the next door.

Fig 8 — Left Hand Door (Inside) — Template — Hinge Rebates — A — B

For right hand wall cupboard doors, simply turn the template over, with "right" upward and repeat the process.

Base cupboard doors can be marked using the same template. The template marked "left" will become the template for right hand doors while the template marked "right" will be for the left hand doors.

FITTING DRAWER HANDLES

Drawer handles can be fitted in a similar manner. You will need to make a new template for drawers using the same method for cupboard doors.

Check all handles to make sure the distance between fixing holes is the same before drilling, although the handles all look the same, some differences may occur.

DUMMY DOORS AND OVEN FILLER PANELS

These items are fitted to the cabinets by means of brackets on the back face of the door or panel. Before fitting either built in appliances or the sink and hob, make sure you will have access to fit brackets. If access is not possible you will need to fit these items first.

Hold the panel in its position against the cabinet, mark a line on the inside of the panel using the cabinet edge as a guide. Fit the brackets flush with the marked line; reposition the panel and mark through the brackets holes for the fixing position. Drill a 2mm pilot hole then fix the panel in position.

APPLIANCES

For washing machines and dishwashers, pass any hoses and power leads through the previously made opening in the adjacent cupboard but do not connect. If heat-shield tape is required for the underside of the worktop, apply it now. Move the appliance into position taking care not to damage the plastic legs. Adjust the legs or feet to the required height, making sure the appliance is level, fit the screws through the bracket and into the worktop or side panel as directed by the instructions. Connect the water supply and open the valves, check for leaks. Connect the drain hose to the waste and plug the appliance in to the mains. If there are no leaks and the power light illuminates, leave testing of the machine until later. If the appliance is freestanding and much lower than the worktop, the space can be utilised for a tray storage shelf using colour matched panelling.

Consult instructions supplied with built in ovens before installing them. Once in place and connected to gas and/or electricity, they are normally secured by two or four screws through the front face of the appliance and into the cabinet side panels.

PLINTHS.

Plinths are fitted to the cabinet legs by means of sliding plastic clips screwed to the inner face of the plinth. A plastic sealing strip is usually applied along the bottom edge of the plinth to prevent any water and dust getting underneath.

When fitting to internal corners (D), the plinth should extend into the corner to allow the furthest cabinet leg to support it. The following description relates to the U shaped layout used throughout this guide.

First, cut the plinth to length, ensuring a clean cut to both ends. Place the plinth in position to check that it will fit under the cabinet. If the plinth is higher than the recess you will need to mark it and cut it to size. Always cut the top of the plinth if it needs adjusting, as the top edge should be invisible once fitted. You may need to cut a 10mm recess to allow the dishwasher door to open, check the instructions supplied with the appliance for actual dimensions. Fit the plinth in the order as described below.

SECTION A

Lay the plinth on the floor in the position that it will be fitted, with the finished face downward. Using a pencil, mark the centre line of each cabinet leg onto the plinth; this is where the plastic clips will be fitted. Screw the clips onto the plinth, central to the marked lines and slide the second part of the clip into position. Lift the plinth and angle it towards the legs and check each clip is directly opposite a leg.

Adjust the clips by sliding them until they are in the correct position. Once in position, gently push the plinth against the legs until you hear it click into place.

SECTION B

Measure the distance between the front face of Section A and either the face of the end panel, or the far edge of the end cabinet. Cut the plinth to length and fit as for Section A. If you were supplied with clips for joining Section A to Section B, fit them as instructed.

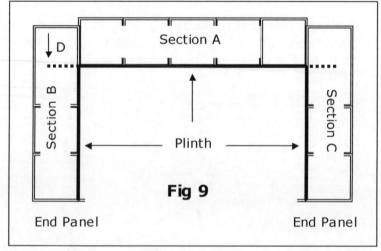

Fig 9

SECTION C

Repeat the process as for Section B

PLINTHS

If you do not have end panels at the end of the run of cabinets, you will need to fit a short length of plinth at this point. Repeat the cutting and marking method as for section A but position the front clip above centre. This is because the front leg will have two clips attached to it.

On some cabinets, the top flange of the leg will prevent the plinth from fitting flush with the side panel. To remedy this, chisel a section of the plinth from the back face until the plinth will sit flush.

If you are fitting plinth to butt up against skirting board, use the scribing methods described in this guide, to ensure a gap free joint. Finally, fit iron on edging to any sawn side edges of the plinth.

CORNICE AND PELMET

Both of these mouldings are cut using either a manual, or power mitre saw, the joints are set with super glue and the whole section is then screwed to the top or bottom of the cupboards.

Ideally a top of the range compound mitre saw is used to cut the mouldings to produce a near invisible joint. However, a good-looking professional joint can still be produced with lesser equipment so long as it is accurate and has a sharp blade.

Depending on the shape of your mouldings, joints are either standard mitres or compound mitres. The difference being that changing the horizontal and vertical angle of the blade produces a compound mitre cut, whereas changing only the horizontal angle produces a standard mitre. If you are unsure which type of cut you require, make a sample corner and check that it will join together at 90°. Consult the instructions supplied with the saw for the setting required to produce mitred or compound mitred joints and practice before cutting your mouldings.

The key to producing successful joints is holding the moulding straight and secure while cutting the joint and always cutting into the front face. Prepare the area first to allow enough space to support a length of the moulding and practice using clamps to secure it. The edge of the moulding that is screwed to the cupboards should always be placed flat on the bed of the mitre saw with the good face of the moulding facing you.

CORNICE AND PELMET

While there are mathematical methods to cut and fit cornice and pelmets, the following trial and error procedure is a successful method for the beginner to follow to produce a good-looking result. The procedure is based on mouldings of 50mm or less and uses only standard 45° joints; it can be adapted for moulding of any size or angle. Practices cutting the joins first – if you can cut a 45° join and set it together with no gaps you only have the measuring to think about next.

Cut the moulding in the order as shown below.

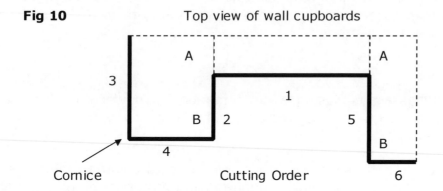

Fig 10   Top view of wall cupboards

Cornice   Cutting Order   6

Section 1 (Fig 10)

Cut sections 2 & 5 with the correct mitre at end A, cut the sections oversize by 75mm* but do not cut the angle at end B yet. Place sections 2 & 5 into the final position and temporarily secure to the top of the cupboard with screws or brackets. Measure dimension C (Fig 10A), add 5mm and mark it onto section 1. Cut the section with the correct mitres at each end and slide it into position from the back, between sections 2 & 5. The section should be just too long to fit, remove the section to trim one angle down, little by little until it is a perfect fit. Temporarily secure section 1 in position using screws or brackets.

* This allowance is to cut the opposite mitre, allow more or less depending on the height of your cornice.

CORNICE AND PELMET

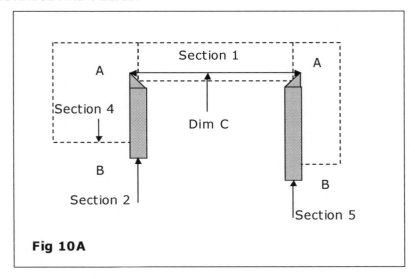

Fig 10A

Section 2

With section 2 still in position, position and cut the mitre to section 4, at end B, again leave this section 75mm oversize and do not cut the angle to the other end. Place the section into position and mark the line for cutting the mitre to section 2, end B. Draw a faint pencil line of the angle to remind you which direction to cut. Remove section 2 and cut the mitre 5mm longer than the marked line. Replace section 2 into position and offer sections 4 up against it. Again using the little by little method, trim section 2 until both sections provide the desired joint.

Sections 3 (Fig 10B)

Measure the distance (D) between the edge of the cabinet and the furthest point of the mitre on section 2. Measure the distance from the wall to the front of the cabinet at 3; add the two measurements together and cut sections 3 to length with the correct mitre. Temporarily fit the section into position with screws or brackets.

CORNICE AND PELMET

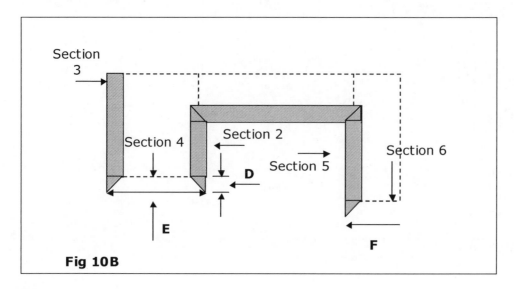

Section 3

Section 4

Section 2

Section 5

D

Section 6

E

F

Fig 10B

Section 4

Measure the distance between the furthest points of section 2 & 3 (E), add 5mm and cut and fit using the little by little trimming method until a perfect joint is achieved.

Section 5

With section 5 still in position, draw a line flush with the edge of the cabinet at end B. Add dimension (D) and cut to length with the correct mitre.

Section 6

Measure the distance between the wall and the furthest point of the mitre on section 5 (F). Cut the section slightly oversize and trim little by little until it is a perfect fit.

With all joints now cut, check each one to ensure a perfect, gap free join. Use fine sandpaper to remove any burrs or rough areas.

The joints will now be assembled in sections and lifted onto the cupboard before the final two joints are glued. Ensure you have a flat area to assemble the joints; an old section of worktop is perfect for this.

The whole 'little by little' process may get tedious but it will ensure that the expensive moulding is not cut incorrectly and wasted.

CORNICE AND PELMET

Assemble sections 2, 3 & 4

Apply a liberal coating of superglue to the mitred face of section 3 and spray the corresponding area of section 4 with superglue activator. Allow approximately 15 seconds for the activator to evaporate then press the joint together. Make sure both sections are perfectly aligned and not twisted in any way, hold firmly in position for 15 seconds until set. Join section 2 to the other end of section 4, you now have a joined U shaped section, place it on top of the cupboards but do not secure it yet.

Assemble section 5 & 6

Assemble these two sections into an L shape and fit to the top of the cupboards using screws or brackets.

Section 1

Place section 1 into position and glue to the fitted section 5 using the above method.

Glue the other end of section 1 into position with section 2 and secure all sections of the cornice to the top of the cupboards.

To join lengths of cornice or pelmet, cut each section with a standard, but opposing 45° mitre and join with super glue and activator. The reason for the mitre cut is to provide a stronger joint and a larger surface area for the glue to bond to.

The same cutting and fitting method is used to fit pelmets and can also be used for any combination of mitres or angles.

CORNICE AND PELMET

Setting and cutting mitres to cornice and pelmets.

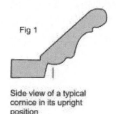

Fig 1

Side view of a typical cornice in its upright position

Cutting mitres to moulded cornice & pelmets is always tricky so take your time and practice first if you have enough moulding to spare. To make the perfect joint there are 2 main factors;

Fig 2

Mitre Saw

Fence

1 -Machine and Blade

A mitre saw similar to the Dewalt DW707 fitted with a sharp 60tpi blade will cut the moulding perfectly. The downside is that you will need to spend around £250 to £300 on the machine. A lesser machine may also cut a near perfect joint but invariably will be slightly inferior to the Dewalt but still be good enough for the untrained eye.

2 – Positioning and cutting

Positioning and cutting the many varied lengths of moulding is critical to ensure a good joint. If you position one slightly differently to the other you will achieve a good join but it will be near impossible to screw the section to the cupboard without the join breaking apart.

Unless you are cutting small 'bull nosed' mouldings which are quite simple to hold you will need to measure and cut an off- cut to ensure consistent positioning and cutting.

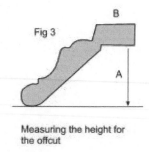

Fig 3

B

A

Measuring the height for the offcut

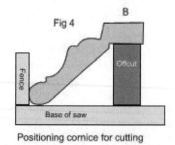

Fig 4

B

Fence

Offcut

Base of saw

Positioning cornice for cutting

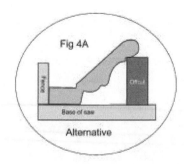

Fig 4A

Fence

Offcut

Base of saw

Alternative

CORNICE AND PELMET

Preparation

The key to a good joint is to make sure the moulding is consistently supported at the correct angle while cutting. The angle is the same as when it is fitted to the cupboard and that is <u>flat</u>. When measuring dimension A from diagram 3 you must make sure that surface B is level and not sloping forward or backward.

Most cornice and pelmet cutting involves long lengths. Prepare supports beforehand to ensure the moulding sits flat on the bed of the mitre saw.
If you can, utilise clamps to help while cutting all the better, but once you have the moulding in the right position and properly supported you will rely on holding it firm with one hand while cutting with the other.

Normally, cutting into the finished face, as Fig 4 will produce a clean, chip free cut. In the unlikely event that your mitre saw behaves differently you may have to position the moulding in the alternative position shown in fig 4A.

Angles and cuts

The angles for cupboards are usually 22.5° or 45 ° and are either a standard mitre cut or a compound mitre cut. A standard mitre cut is with the blade positioned vertically but set at an angle of 22.5° or 45 °. A compound mitre cut is with the blade tilted at the desired angle (/ or \ )and also set at an angle to cut the mitre.

You will need to determine which angle and which cut you will need for your mouldings and you can do this by practicing first. It is quite easy to use up lots of moulding by practising so it's better to use spare timber or preferably, the moulding from your old kitchen until you know the correct angle and cut.

The Cutting Process

Position the moulding against the fence of the saw as Fig 4. Position the off cut as Fig 4 making sure it is clear of the blade when you cut the moulding. If the off cut is the correct height and the moulding is supported along the length, the face B should be level. Hold the moulding and the off cut firmly while cutting and do not push down on the saw, let the blade do the work and it should not move the moulding while cutting.
Calculate the next angle to cut, set the mitre saw and repeat the above process. Test the joint by holding both sections together on a flat surface. The join should meet along the length of the cut while both sections of moulding remain flat on the surface.
If you have cut the joint and it doesn't join you can re-cut one or both mitres again by removing 1 or 2mm. It shouldn't make too much difference when fitted.

13 - HOW TO

1 - FIT A WORKTOP WITH JOINING STRIPS

Joining strips are a simple and effective method for joining worktops, either at corners or in straight lengths. Corner joining strips have one curved face, which sits over the rounded edge, and one flat face, which screws flush to the edge of the adjoining worktop. Joining strips for connecting straight sections of worktop together are T shaped and simply fit between the 2 straight edges of a worktop. (Fig 11)

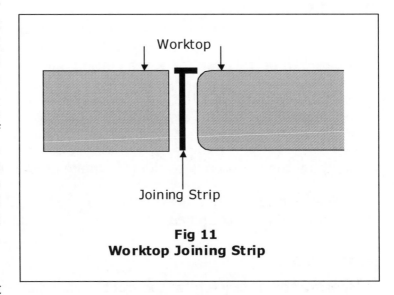

Fig 11
Worktop Joining Strip

It is important to ensure that all sawn edges of the worktop are cut straight and clean when using jointing strips. Preparing worktops for edging strips can be achieved with the use of a good quality handsaw, however, the preferred method is with a router as described in part 3 of the 'How To' section.

Joining strips save the time and expense of cutting and fitting mitred joints, the disadvantage to this way of joining worktops is that the strip sits proud of the worktop and is visible. This can be minimised by purchasing colour co-ordinated joining strips at the time you buy your worktop.

The fitted worktop described in this section is for a U shaped section as Fig 12.

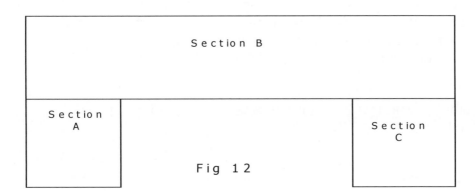

1 - FIT A WORKTOP USING ALUMINIUM JOINING STRIPS

SECTION B

Measure the length of worktop required for section B and deduct 4mm, this will allow a 2mm fitting gap on sides A & C. Apply masking tape to the area of the worktop to be cut, and mark the cutting lines in pencil.

Place the worktop on the workbenches and hold secure with clamps. Cut along the lines with a jigsaw ensuring that both pieces of the worktop will be supported on workbenches once cut.

Next, lay the worktop in position to make certain it fits.

If clean straight edges are required on section B, refer to part 3 of the 'How To' section of this book and cut the edges with a router.

SECTION A & C

Measure the distance from the front rounded edge of the worktop section B to the end of your worktop run, add 50mm to the length for trimming and cut the worktop square, either with a handsaw or router.

If you have a larder unit or return wall at the end of the run of cupboards see part 2 of the 'How To' section for the cutting procedure.

Apply a thin film of clear silicone sealant to the cut edge of section A where the joining strip will be attached and screw the strip to the worktop edge.

Lay the worktop in position so the curved face of the joining strip sits over the rounded edge of section B and make sure it fits well.

To trim the worktop to length - draw a pencil line on the underside of the worktop flush with the top end of the run of cupboards; this will give the finished length of the worktop. If your worktop includes an overhang, add the overhang measurement to the pencil line. Cut this line with either a handsaw or for a perfectly straight cut, use a router. (See part 3 of the 'How To' section of this book)

Apply sealant to the inside, rounded face of the joining strip and set the worktop into its final position.

To secure the worktop to the cupboards, drill one pilot hole through each of the top rails of the base cupboards and screw through into the worktop.

2 - CUT WORKTOP TO LENGTH IF LARDERS OR RETURN WALLS ARE IN THE WAY

For worktops that do not allow trimming to size afterwards, the following is a proven procedure

If the angle between the wall and the larder unit/return wall is not 90° you will need to, either, use an angle devisor or produce a template of the angle.

To produce a template of the angle, use a piece of spare packing cardboard with at least one long straight edge and an equal width to the worktop. Position the longest edge of the cardboard against the wall and butt the other edge against the larder unit/return wall. Trim the cardboard to suit the angle of the larder unit/return wall; this is the template and can then be transferred to the worktop for cutting.

Next, place two off cuts of worktop on top of the base units; lay the prepared length of worktop on top of the off cuts ensuring the angled end fits snugly against the larder unit/return wall and the other end is laying over the rounded edge of section B.

Working from below the worktop, make 2 marks on the underside of the worktop using the rounded edge of section B as a guide, deduct 2mm (the thickness of the joining strip) from these marks and draw a line between them. This will be your cutting line and ensures a perfect fit every time.

3 - USE A ROUTER TO PRODUCE STRAIGHT, CLEAN-CUT EDGES

Only cut from left to right with the router at depths of 15mm per cut. Only cut into the rounded edge of the worktop. Cutting against the direction of the router will damage the blade and chip the worktop. Always use a sharp blade.

Routers used for producing mitred joins in worktops are fitted with a 30mm guide bush and a 12.7mm blade. For this reason, you cannot cut a marked line without first offsetting the jig to accommodate the guide bush. (See instructions supplied with your jig for further information) In this case the offset is 9mm, this should be applied to every cut made with the router.

CUTTING A STRAIGHT LINE.

Mark the position of the line to be cut on the worktop. Draw another line 9mm back from this line; this will be your guideline. Set the jig on the worktop so that the back edge of the cutting slot aligns with the guideline. Clamp the jig to the worktop and place the router in the cutting slot 50mm in from the left hand side of the worktop.

3 - USE A ROUTER TO PRODUCE STRAIGHT, CLEAN-CUT EDGES

CUTTING A STRAIGHT LINE.

Start the router and plunge downward 50mm in from the left hand edge until the cutter just marks the surface. Repeat this, 50mm in from the right hand edge. If you have set the jig correctly both cutter marks will be exactly on the cutting line. If so, proceed with the cut at depths of 15mm, if not, readjust the jig until correct. Finally, use fine grade sandpaper to remove frayed lining paper from the underside edge of the worktop.

4 - FIT WORKTOPS TO OUT OF SQUARE WALLS

Maintaining an even overhang from the rounded edge of the worktop to the front edge of cabinets is the key to successful worktop fitting. Standard 600mm wide worktop should overhang a standard 560mm cabinet by 40mm. On kitchens that have square corners and flat walls it is not difficult to achieve this, plus or minus 5mm, along each length of the worktops.

Many kitchens, however, do not have square corners or perfectly straight walls, which means that worktops will require scribing to fit snugly against the wall. If neither tiles nor splash backs are to be fixed once the worktop is fitted, the largest gap should be no more than 3mm, this gap can be concealed with silicone sealant at the finishing off stage. If you plan to tile the walls or add a splash back once the worktop is fitted, the thickness of the tiles or splash back and a bead of silicone could cover many gaps. Decide for yourself whether the worktop needs to be scribed and cut to fit the wall.

Remember, when you fitted the base cabinets to the wall, the furthest point that they project from the wall is the width of the worktop minus 40mm (in this case 560mm). When you scribe a worktop you will be cutting a section of the worktop away that allows the worktop to move in towards the wall to achieve the 40mm overhang. If it appears that you will cut so much of the worktop away that the overhang will be much less than 40mm you will need to remedy the wall rather than the worktop. This would only be necessary on a severely bowed wall and should have been catered for during the planning stage.

Again, this section is based upon the U shaped configuration as shown but with uneven walls and out of square corners.

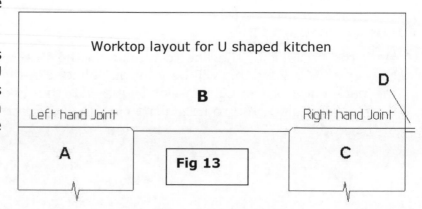

Worktop layout for U shaped kitchen

Left hand Joint

Right hand Joint

B

D

A

Fig 13

C

4 - FIT WORKTOPS TO OUT OF SQUARE WALLS

SCRIBING SECTION B

To cut section B to length will require at template produced for each end of the worktop (Fig 13A). To do this, place a large square of the packing cardboard on top of the cabinets and into each corner, and then scribe the wall contours onto it using a compass and pencil.

Make a mark on each side wall and both templates, 300mm in from the back wall. Also make a mark on the worktop, 300mm in from the back straight edge.

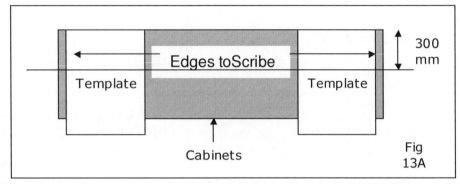

Fig 13A

Transfer and mark one of the contours to the equivalent end of the worktop and cut along the line.

Measures the distance between the two marks made at 300mm on the sidewalls and deduct 4mm to allow for fitting sides A & C.

From the side of the worktop that has already been scribed, transfer this measurement to the worktop, 300mm in from the back straight edge. Align the mark on the second template with this point and draw the contour onto the worktop before cutting the line. When the worktop is set into position it should have 2mm flexibility at either end.

TO SCRIBE THE BACK EDGE OF THE WORKTOP

With the worktop in place, set the overhang of the worktop to be equal along the front edge of the cabinets.

Apply a strip of 50mm masking tape along the top, back edge of the worktop.

Measure the depth of the worktop overhang. Remember, the target overhang to aim for is 40mm. If the current overhang is 50mm, you will need to set your compass to a width of 10mm (current overhang 50mm, minus target of 40mm = 10mm)

4 - FIT WORKTOPS TO OUT OF SQUARE WALLS

TO SCRIBE THE BACK EDGE OF THE WORKTOP

With the compass set to the desired width, run the point of the compass along the back wall, this will in turn draw a line on the masking tape to the exact shape of the back wall. Cut along the line with a jigsaw and the worktop should now fit against the wall with minimal gaps and a 40mm overhang.

Next, cut the left and right female mitred joints; see Fitting Your Own Kitchen – Stage 3

CUTTING SECTION A

Place an off cut of worktop on top of the cabinets at the end of the run of cabinets

Cut Section A, 75mm longer than the required finished length of the worktop. Place it in position on top of the off cut and lying over the mitred joint of section B by 50mm and ensure an even overhang along the length.

Measure the distance between the start of the mitre in section B and the face of the rounded edge of section A. This will be the dimension to set your compass and scribe the back edge of the worktop. Cut along the scribed line and place the worktop back in the same position. From below the cabinets, mark a line on the underside of the worktop along the edge of the female mitre. This will be the cutting line for the male joint. Remove the worktop and cut the left hand male joint; see Fitting Your Own Kitchen – Stage 3.

SECTION C

Repeat the above process for scribing and cutting section A of the worktop.

You may find it as easy to chop some sections of the plaster away at worktop level, rather than to cut the worktop to allow it to sit slightly into the wall.

5 – PLUMB THE SINK AND APPLIANCES

This section will deal with the simplest way to plumb your kitchen. The advice is aimed at those new to plumbing. If you have had experience at plumbing you can use any fittings you choose to achieve the end result.

For the purposes of installing a kitchen you should aim to have all water and waste connections prepared before you fix the cabinets to the wall. It is easier to cut a section from the service area of a cabinet while fitting it than to try to fit pipes through it afterwards. Ideally you will aim at leaving both water supply pipes and waste pipe ready for connecting once the sink is installed.

DRAINAGE

Washing machines, sinks and dishwashers all require pipe work to enable wastewater to drain away. The easiest way to cope with washing machine and dishwasher waste is to use a U bend fitting on the sink with connections for the appliance waste. The hoses from the appliances are then simply clamped to the inlet on the U bend fitting.

Follow manufactures instructions to set the height of waste hoses before they connect to U bends.

If the appliances are too far way from the sink to utilise the U bend fitting, you will need to install new waste pipes that either connect into the main waste behind the sink or exit through the wall into a drain outside.

All new pipe work should be of 40mm diameter and fitted in such a way that it is sloping downwards and away from the appliance. Each appliance will require its own washing machine trap if not connected to the sink U bend; these are widely available from plumbing suppliers. Washing machine traps should be positioned in a cupboard adjoining the appliance, do not fit them behind the appliance, as it will cause the appliance to protrude beyond the line of the worktop.

If you decide to install new pipe work for the waste, I recommend the use of solvent weld connectors and pipe. These are plastic components that can easily be configured for most applications. The advantage of solvent weld components is that you can assemble your system to make sure it all fits before disassembling and applying the solvent adhesive. If all pipes are cut squarely when using these fittings, it is highly unlikely that you will encounter a leak. See Shopping List section for details.

5 - PLUMB THE SINK AND APPLIANCES

WATER SUPPLY CONNECTIONS

For the novice plumber I would recommend using a combination of push fit fittings, copper pipe and flexible braided hoses as there really is nothing to be gained by making the plumbing more complicated.

For a standard (Fig 14) kitchen containing a sink, dishwasher and washing machine you will need the following components:

2 Flexible braided push fit hoses to suit your tap connection

4 Push fit washing machine taps (if each appliance require both hot and cold feed)

4 Push fit T connectors

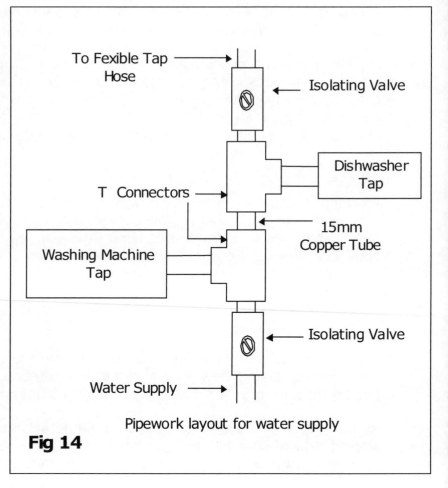

Fig 14

Pipework layout for water supply

4 Push fit quarter turn isolating valves

Configured as Fig 14 to each of the supply pipes:

The connectors are joined to each other using 50mm lengths of copper tube.

This configuration is simple and will allow you to shut either individual water supplies off, or all supplies off with a simple turn of a valve.

For appliances that are too far away to connect below the sink you will need to extend the T connector branches to be sited close to the appliance. Again, make these connections inside and adjoining cupboard rather than behind the appliance.

6 - SCRIBE END PANELS

Where end panels are visible at the end of a run of cupboards, you may need to scribe them to fit tightly against the back wall. It is quite simple to scribe end panels and will provide a more professional look to the finished kitchen.

First decide if the gap (if there is one) between the end panel and the wall requires scribing. For gaps of 2-3mm's I would advise finishing off with silicone sealant. For larger gaps you will need to scribe the panels as follows.

Make sure the cabinet it set to its finished height and is level on all planes. Place it up against the adjacent cabinet but sitting 25mm forward of the front edge, clamp it in this position and apply masking tape along the length of the back edge. Set your compass to 25mm and run the point down the back wall transferring the contour to the cabinet side panel. Cut along the line with a jigsaw and refit the cabinet, it will now fit perfectly.

7 - CUTTING AND SAWING TIPS

Nothing looks worse on a new kitchen than chipped laminate edges caused by careless cutting. The following guidelines will produce clean straight edges every time with no missing laminate.

As a rule, apply 50mm masking tape to every cut you make with a jigsaw or handsaw. This serves two purposes, the first is that you will be able to see the cutting line clearly, and the second is to ensure no laminate breaks loose. Don't be tempted to scrimp and use 25mm tape, as it will lift off during the cutting process. Do not use masking tape on cuts made with a router, if necessary, use two 25mm strips and mark the position of the line onto it, you can then align the jig between these marks.

LAMINATED WORKTOPS

Jigsaw – cut the worktop face up with a laminate cutting blade. Note - it is difficult to obtain a perfectly straight edge with a jigsaw, if it is critical for the edge to be clean and straight I would recommend cutting with a handsaw or even better, a router.

Handsaw – always cut the worktop with the face upwards.

Router – only ever cut into the rounded edge of worktop with a router. The joint that you are cutting will determine whether the worktop is cut face up or face down.

7 - CUTTING AND SAWING TIPS

SAWING END PANELS, PLINTHS AND CABINET CUT OUTS

Cut with the good face upward, either with a jigsaw fitted with a laminate cutting blade or handsaw.

8 – CUT AND FIT FILLET PANELS

Many kitchens require fillet panels to cover small gaps between cabinets or between cabinets and the wall. Although these are a tiny part of the kitchen they are big enough to make or break the professional look you are endeavouring to produce. The extra care taken when measuring and cutting fillets will be reflected in the finished result.

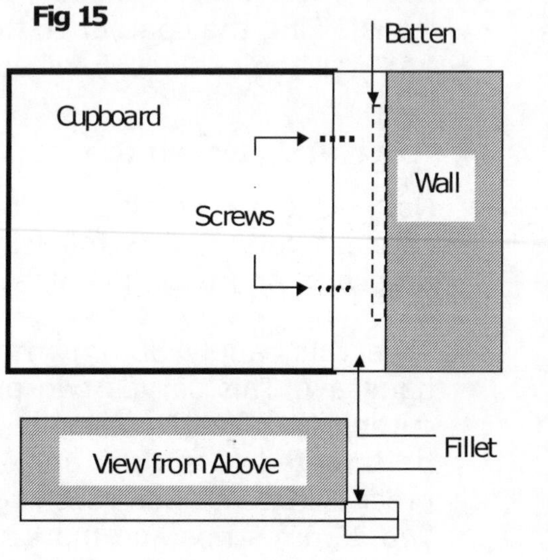

CUTTING AND FIXING FILLET PANELS BETWEEN CABINETS AND WALLS (FIG 15)

The finished face of the fillet should always be flush with the cabinet door to give the appearance of a designed finish rather than a part added to fill a gap.

To achieve this you will cut the fillet from a section of colour-matched panel that also has the colour matching on one side edge. You will also cut a piece slightly smaller than the fillet, which will be used for fixing to the cabinet. This piece can be cut from old end panels and does not need to be colour matched. The colour-matched edge will face the cabinet and the sawn edge will face the wall.

Fig 15

Measure and cut a fillet to fit the gap exactly from the colour-matched panel. If the wall is irregular you will need to make a template and scribe the panel before cutting.

Cut a copy of this fillet, 2mm (approx) narrower and from and old end panel.

Align the fillets on top of each other and screw through the copy into the fillet so that you have a double thickness fillet. The narrower edge of the copy will be closest to the wall.

If the fillet is less than 50mm wide it can be held in place by screws through the cabinet. If it is much wider you will need to secure a batten to the wall to support it.

CUTTING AND FIXING FILLET PANELS BETWEEN CABINETS AND WALLS

Place the fillet in position with the long edge of the copy against the long edge of the cabinet; this will allow the colour matched fillet to sit proud of the cabinet and flush with the door. Mark a line on the wall behind the fillet if required, this will be the line for attaching a batten. The batten can be held to the wall with adhesive if you do not want to remove the wall cupboard to drill and fix raw plugs.

When you are ready to fit the fillet, remove cabinet door hinges and mid shelf and drill 2.5mm pilot holes, 6mm in from the cupboard edge. Screw through these holes into the fillet ensuring it is flush with the top and bottom of the cabinets. Replace the hinges and shelf to cover the screw heads.

If a batten is fitted for support, the fillet can either be secured at the back with a bracket or fixed with adhesive.

CUTTING AND FIXING FILLETS BETWEEN CABINETS

These fillets are best cut and fitted as a single thickness piece between the cabinet edges. This is because you need a colour-matched panel with both edges laminated to be able to fit them as the above method. It is possible to use iron on edging to make a good edge but experience shows that these do not last.

Simply cut a fillet to size from colour-matched panel and screw through each side of the cabinet, behind the hinges, to secure.

9 - FIT BASE CABINETS TO IRREGULAR WALLS OR OUT OF SQUARE KITCHENS

If you have checked the corners of your kitchen and discovered that they are not quite square, you will not be surprised to find that your cornet cabinet will not fit snugly to each side wall.

To remedy either this problem or the dilemma of irregularly shaped walls you will need to make modifications to the service void at the back of some of the units as follows.

IRREGULAR WALLS

Place the corner cabinet in position and level it to the finished height.

If the back edges of the side panels rest against the wall at the top but not at the bottom it is not necessary to correct the problem. Remember, the maximum dimension the top of the cabinet can protrude from the wall is, worktop width minus 40mm. This is to maintain an even overhang when the worktop is fitted.

9 – FIT BASE CABINETS TO IRREGULAR WALLS OR OUT OF SQUARE KITCHENS

IRREGULAR WALLS

If you prefer to know that the cupboards are properly fitted you can scribe the edges of the cupboard at the service void section and cut along the line. This will produce perfectly fitted cupboards.

If however, the bottom edges of the side panels touch the wall but not the top, you will have to modify the service void until the top edges are against the wall. There are two options for this; firstly you can simply cut away 80% of the service void, this will allow the whole cupboard to move inward at the bottom and solve the problem. The second option is to scribe both side panels of the cupboard at the service void section and cut along the line. This will allow the cupboard to fit against the wall without gaps.

Whichever option you choose, you may have to repeat the process with adjoining cupboards and also scribe the worktop.

OUT OF SQUARE

If the corner unit does not sit squarely into the corner you will need to cut one or all of the service voids to size. Using a combination square, ensure that the cupboard is at 90° to both walls once you have adjusted it.

For a purpose built corner unit it is generally the service void of the back panel at the centre of the cupboard that will require trimming. For corner units constructed from two standard cupboards, the service voids to be trimmed will be those nearest the corner. Trim these equally to ensure the cupboard remains at 90° to the wall.

If you are unfortunate enough to have both, out of square corners and irregular walls you will need to combine each of the above solutions.

Again, you may have to trim the service voids of adjacent cupboards if you modify the corner unit.

WALL CUPBOARDS

Wall cupboards cannot be modified in the same manner of base cupboards, as they do not have a service void as such. Cupboards fitted with adjustable brackets can be adjusted inward and outward by means of one of the screws in the suspension bracket to alleviate fitting to out of square corners. Uneven walls are either best treated before fitting the kitchen or disguised with end panels and tiles to hide any unsightly gaps.

10 - FIT 2 PIECE CORNER CABINETS.

2 piece corner units are simply 2 cabinets (base or wall) or appliances, positioned and joined together by a corner post. The common factor for a 2-piece corner unit is the corner post, C and the dimension X. (Fig 16)

After studying Fig 16, you will be aware of the purpose of the corner post. One function is to act as a spacer to enable doors or drawers on either cupboard to be opened without hitting the door or handle of the cupboard next to it; the other is to achieve a built in look to the corners.

Fig 16 is for reference; check your plan for the configuration of cabinets suitable for your kitchen.

To install the cabinets; first consult the instructions supplied with the cabinet or corner post to determine the dimension X.

Measure the width of the door to be fitted to Cabinet B, add 3mm and make a mark on the top and bottom front edges of the cabinet as indicated by D. (Fig 16)

Fit the corner post to cabinet A, screw two brackets to the back of the post and fit it so that the face of the corner post will be flush with the proposed door.

Place cabinet B into position, the required distance (X) from the wall.

Set cabinet A into position and ensure the whole assembly is square.

Drill and screw through the back of the centre support post of cabinet B and into the corner post to join the two cabinets together.

Ensure both units are still set at the correct height and level, and then secure both cabinets to the wall.

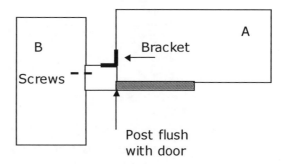

10 - FIT 2 PIECE CORNER CABINETS.

The following diagram is of one configuration of the corner unit. There are two configuration options for each corner, as shown in Fig 17

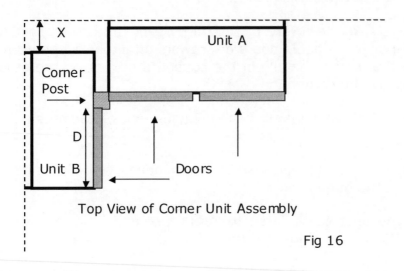

Top View of Corner Unit Assembly

Fig 16

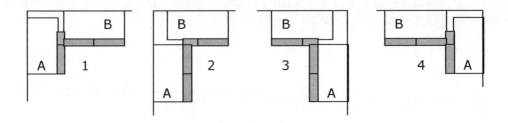

Fig 17 - Corner Unit Combinations

If the assembly cannot be fitted squarely, consult the scribing section of this guide to modify the service void panels. The above method of fitting is suitable for both base and wall units.

11 - SEAL THE WORKTOP

Applying silicone sealant to the back and sides of the worktop is a job that is critical to get looking good. After all the effort of fitting your kitchen the last thing you want is to spoil the look with a thick line of unsightly sealant.

If you are not adept with a sealant gun, the best way to neatly apply sealant is to use 50mm masking tape to mask the worktop and tiles. Apply the tape to the worktop as close to the edge as possible, keep it straight and make sure the edge is stuck down all the way along. Apply another strip of tape to the wall or tiles, again as close as possible to the worktop; this will leave a small area between the wall and worktop for the sealant to be applied. Next, run the sealant gun along the length of the masked off area, applying enough, but not too much sealant to the gap. Wet your finger and run it along the gap,

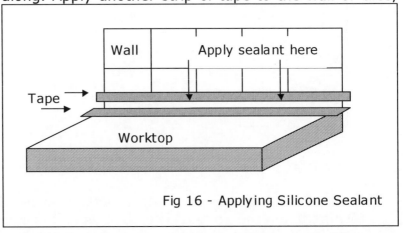

Fig 16 - Applying Silicone Sealant

shaping the sealant as you go and forcing any excess onto the taped edges. As soon as you have a smooth finish along the length of the worktop, remove the tape for a perfect finish. This method can also be used for sealing between walls and side panels.

12 - BISCUIT JOINTING

Biscuit joints comprise of slots machined into each cut face of the worktop exactly opposite each other. Oval, wooden "biscuits" are then fitted to the slots and glued into place while joining the worktop.

This type of joint will ensure a flush fit to all edges of the worktop once joined. Biscuit joints are used in conjunction with worktop bolts therefore they should be marked and cut between bolt recesses.

12 - BISCUIT JOINTING

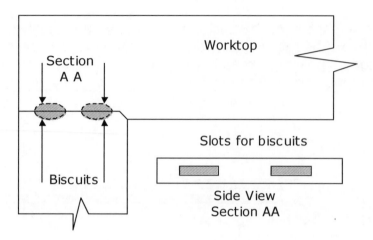

Fig 16 - Biscuit Jointing

The joints can either be cut with a dedicated biscuit cutter machine, or with an attachment for the router. The joint is not suitable for every corner joint as clearance on at least one side is required when assembling it.

13 – FIT CABINET BACK PANELS

Back panels that require modifying to allow for obstructions can usually be cut before the cabinet is secured to the wall. Some panels however, can only be fitted afterwards, depending on the level of obstruction. This applies mainly to the sink unit containing the plumbing etc.

There are two options to fit the panels once all pipe work connections are complete, they are;

Trim approximately one third from the height of the panel and try to locate it in the panel grooves at the back of the cupboard. Cut holes or shapes for access to isolation valves beforehand. The panels are quite flexible and will allow an amount of bending to get them into place.

If the majority of the pipe work sits forward of the grooves in the cabinet you will need to make a frame to set the back panel further forward.

13 – FIT CABINET BACK PANELS

Attach 12mm square battens to the sides and base of the cabinet on the inside of the cabinet, flush with the furthest point of the obstruction. Trim the width of the back panel to exactly the width of the cupboard. Trim an amount from the top panel, normally a third of the height but your situation will determine how much. Place the modified panel against the batten and mark and cut access holes for isolation valves etc. Screw the panel to the batten bearing in mind that the panel should be easily removable if needed. If you choose this method of modification you may also need to trim the width of the shelf to size.

14 – CONFIGURE SHELVES FOR TALL APPLIANCE UNITS

To successfully fit a tall unit with an appliance fitted into it can be confusing to get right at the first attempt. This is due to conflicting information from the cabinet instructions and those for the appliance. The confusion is usually regarding the shelf height positions as these vary by appliance. The problem is easiest solved during the assembly stage while the cabinet is on the floor, as follows.

Using the plan for the kitchen, identify and unpack the doors and filler panels for the unit. Lay each door on the unit in the position shown in your plan; then lightly mark the position of the top and bottom of each door on the front side panels. The marks will determine the line for the top or bottom of each shelf. Fit the shelves into position, adding appliance support brackets if required then store the doors away for later use.

While this method is generally foolproof, another option is to measure the height of the appliance and doors and calculate the shelf positions.

The positioning of the appliance support shelf will depend on your appliance.

If your appliance sits flush on it base, the shelf will be fitted with its top to the line.

If the appliance has a recess to its front edge the shelf will be fitted with its bottom to the line.

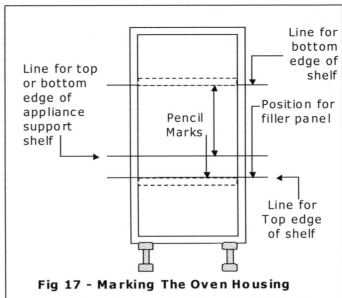

Fig 17 - Marking The Oven Housing

14 – SHOPPING LIST

The following is a list of consumable items that you may need to complete the fitting of your kitchen. The reference numbers on the right are from a company called Screwfix. These are an online and telephone supplier and I rate them as the best for price and delivery. If you visit their website at Screwfix.com and type in a reference number from below, you will see more details, as well as a picture of the product. Some items are only sold in bulk quantities so it may be more economical to buy them locally. Other items are cheaper than you will find in most places; delivery is next day too!

Description	Screwfix Reference	Screwfix Reference	Screwfix Reference
Flexible Tap Hoses	10857	13143	
¼ Turn Isolating Valves	10931	67670	
Washing Machine Taps	18908	25555	
15mm Copper Pipe	31854		
15mm T Connectors	74470	45755	
U Bend(s)	12794	10970	
40mm Solvent Weld Pipe	19477		
40mm Solvent Weld Connectors	90596	99915	35521
Washing Machine Traps	18640		
PTFE Tape	79726		
Solvent Weld Adhesive	14295		
Pipe clips	11880	71879	
Worktop End Protectors	56970		
Worktop Bolts	15295		

Description	Screwfix Reference	Screwfix Reference	Screwfix Reference
Super Glue	14665		
Super Glue Activator	22117		
Masking Tape	16588		
L Brackets	11529	11013	
Drill bits			
Pilot Hole Drill	13841		
4mm HSS Drill	12986		
Impact Adhesive	38770		
Rawplugs	As required		
Screws	As required		
Masonry drill bits	As required		

Where two reference numbers are quoted, they are usually indicating alternatives or options.

Screwfix may well change the products or reference number since publication.

15 - TOOLS REQUIRED

While some tools are unique to kitchen fitting, most are not. The tools listed below are my recommended minimum to fit your kitchen. If you don't own all of the listed tools, you can either hire them or beg or borrow from your friends. Remember, the better the tool you have the better the finished result.

WORKTOP JIG, ROUTER WITH 12.7MM CUTTER & CLAMPS

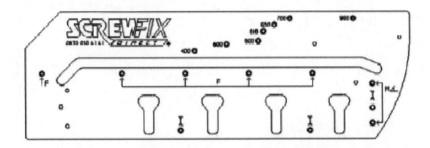

The above is a typical, suitable worktop jig, available from Screwfix (18953). If you are planning to buy your own jig, make sure it is capable of cutting a range of work top widths, including your own! Make sure any jig you buy is supplied with positioning pegs and full instructions.

Routers need to be able to accommodate a ½" cutter and be fitted with a 30 mm guide bush to suit the worktop jig. A minimum of 2 soft-faced clamps are also essential.

If you are fitting your worktop with mitred joints, these items are essential. It is more economical to hire these items unless you are planning to make a living from kitchen fitting. Make sure the router is of appropriate power and that the jig is suitable for the width of your worktop.

WORKBENCHES
At least three of the same height are required if cutting long lengths of worktop

COMBINATION SQUARE
Essential for measuring corners and marking worktop etc

TAPE MEASURES & PENCILS
More than one of each is handy

SCREWDRIVERS
A selection of flat and cross-headed, medium to large, battery or manual

MITRE SAW
Power or manual, for cutting cornice and pelmets

SPIRIT LEVELS
Ideally, one 600mm and one 1metre +

HAMMERS
A claw hammer and a soft-faced hammer if available

FILE
Fine grade for use on laminate ends

COMPASS WITH PENCIL
If you plan to scribe your worktop or cabinets

JIGSAW
Equipped with laminate cutting blades, one fine and one medium

STANLEY KNIFE

HANDSAW
A sharp medium cut for cutting worktop and other laminates

ADJUSTABLE SPANNERS
Two required for plumbing work

HACKSAW
For plumbing work and cutting worktop end caps

TAPES
Electrical, masking and PTFE

DRILLS
Suitable for drilling into brick if needed

DRILL BITS
Wood, 2 & 4mm, masonry as required

PLIERS
Always useful for removing dowels

EXTENSION LEAD

CABLE DETECTOR
Priceless!

10MM SPANNER
For worktop bolts

SEALANT GUN

CHISEL
Medium width blade and sharp, for cutting odd areas

SAFETY EQUIPMENT
Mask, Goggles and Gloves at the minimum

These are the minimum tools that you will need to fit your kitchen. Specialist tools such as Biscuit Cutters, Circular Saws, and Plastic Pipe Cutters etc, while nice to have, are not a necessity.

16 – MEASURING THE KITCHEN

Measuring the kitchen correctly can be helpful to enable you to draw out a rough plan of the kitchen before involving suppliers. Most large suppliers provide free catalogues with cabinet designs and dimensions allowing you to get a good idea of the look and layout at an early stage.

Measure the height of the ceiling to determine which size of wall cabinets will suit your room. A space of 500mm is recommended between the worktop and the bottom of the wall cupboards and a minimum of 20mm is required at the top to allow the wall cupboards to be hooked on to the hanging brackets.

Draw the shape of your kitchen onto some squared or graph paper and add the major dimensions as you go. Measure and mark the position of the doors and windows and then add distances from these openings to corners or wall ends. Measure the distance from the window sill down to the floor and also the height available above the window.

Measure and mark the positions of any visible pipe-work, boxed in areas, serving hatches, air vents and other obstructions or protrusions.

Look below or behind base cabinets to trace any pipe work fitted and draw a dotted line of these on your plan. Ideally you do not want pipes behind your appliances in the new kitchen so they may have to be modified.

Check the angle of each corner; ideally they should be 90°, particularly at the level of the wall corner cupboard if fitted. While worktops and base cabinets can be scribed to fit out of square corners it is much more difficult to fit a corner wall cupboard. Plan to rectify any defective angles above worktop height before fitting the kitchen if possible. To check the angle, simply hold a large square of cardboard into the corner and look for large gaps on one or both sides.

Finally, check the floor levels; use a long spirit level and place it on the floor, 600mm from the wall (the position of the plinth). Find and mark the location of the highest and the lowest point of the floor and measure the distance between them. A dimension of over 20mm will most likely require that the floor be re levelled before fitting any base cabinets.

Once you have measured and drawn all of the above information, make some copies of your plan and try out different configurations before choosing the best one and passing it to the kitchen supplier for verification.

Cutting & Joining Worktops

A Guide To Cutting Mitred Joints

Forethoughts

The theory of cutting worktops is quite simple, you set the jig in the correct position, clamp it down and cut along a preformed slot with a router and hey presto you have a perfect joint!

The reality of cutting worktop joints is only complicated by the fact that you may not have experience of using the tools required or knowledge enough to understand which way round the jig goes and which way up the worktop should be while cutting it. That is why this section is called forethoughts; the more time you spend thinking about cutting the worktops the better your joint will be. An added difficulty is that you will probably only be able to put your theory into practice when it comes to cutting your own worktop so it is unlikely that you will have a trial run.

That said, if you follow the advice from this guide and the instructions supplied with your jig you should be able to produce a very professional looking joint that will last the lifetime of the kitchen.

When cutting into worktops with a rounded edge using a router <u>you can only cut into the rounded edge</u>. This prevents any of the laminate from spitting or chipping but it also means that one joint will be cut with the laminate face upwards and the other with the worktop turned upside down. The main point to remember when using a router is that first contact of the router blade will be into the rounded edge of the worktop. <u>Remember – if the first point of contact the router has with the worktop is the square (back) edge you have the wrong set up</u>

The pictures of cutting worktop in this guide have been taken with the laminate face upwards, this is only for clarity reasons and you should remember that if you cut one half of the joint with the laminate face upward you will need to turn the worktop over when you cut the second of the joints.

Note!
Cut worktops outside if possible as they produce vast amounts of sawdust.
Wear goggles and a mask while cutting for the reason stated above
Do not switch the router on while it is in contact with the worktop or jig
Do not remove the router until the blade has stopped turning
Make sure the cable is out of the way and that clamps will not interfere with cutting

The Tools

Good professional looking joints can be achieved with relatively inexpensive tools and all of them are widely available from on-line suppliers and DIY stores. If you plan to use the tools for a career in kitchen fitting you should choose the more expensive tools as they usually last longer than the DIY tools

The main tools for cutting and joining worktops are;
Router
This needs to be able to accommodate a 12.7mm cutter and should have a power rating of no less than 1600W. You will also need a 30mm guide bush which is an attachment that is fitted to the router for use with the jig.
Jig
Worktop jigs are commonly available and start at very reasonable prices – the main criteria for your jig is that it is suitable for the width of worktop you are cutting. Most are adjustable but do check with the supplier first.
Clamps
At least two good clamps are required to hold the jig and worktop securely while cutting.
Workbenches
A minimum of two, ideally three for long lengths of worktop
A Builders Square
Or similar

See www.diykitchenfitting.co.uk for a full list of tools

Which Joint?

Below are 4 different joints you may need to cut depending on your kitchen layout. As mentioned earlier, some joints are cut with the laminate face upwards and some are cut with the reverse side upwards.

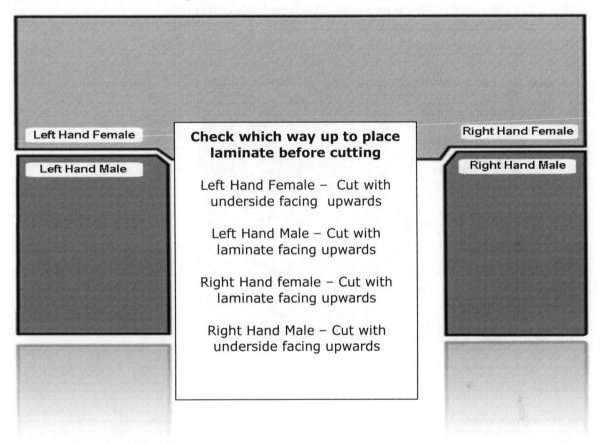

Left Hand Female

Left Hand Male

Right Hand Female

Right Hand Male

Check which way up to place laminate before cutting

Left Hand Female – Cut with underside facing upwards

Left Hand Male – Cut with laminate facing upwards

Right Hand female – Cut with laminate facing upwards

Right Hand Male – Cut with underside facing upwards

The configuration shown above is the most common in kitchens as the joints are as far away from the sink as possible and it is the easiest to measure and cut. You may use any configuration of joints as you wish but they will each compose of a male and female as above.

Look at the diagram above and decide which joint you need to cut then check the chart to see which way up you need to place the worktop while cutting it.
Mark on the worktop the outline of the expected joint as it is easy to get confused and you could cut the wrong type of joint.

Setting the jig to cut male joints

The layout below will cut a left hand male joint
To cut a right hand male joint the setup will be the same but the worktop will be turned over with the chipboard face upwards. The jig will also be turned over and the pegs placed in the same holes but from the otherside.
Male joints are always cut across the width of the worktop
See 'Which Joint' to determine which joint you need to cut

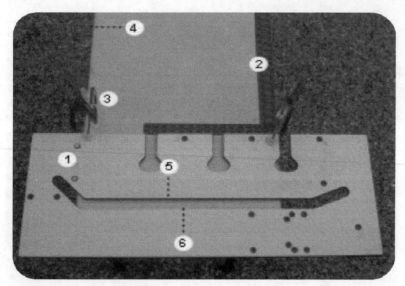

1 – Pegs
2 – Builders Square
3 – Clamps
4 – Rounded Edge
5 – Front Face
6 – Back Face

1 – Place two pegs in the holes as illustrated, usually market 'M' for male – make sure the pegs are flush with the surface of the jig so that they do not interfere with the path of the router.
2 - Position a builders square or similar tool along the back straight edge of the worktop to ensure the jig is at 90°
3 – Use 2 clamps to hold the jig to the worktop and workbenches making sure they will not be in the way once you start routing. If the worktop is a long length and supported by a workbench at the other end, apply another 2 clamps to that end.
4- Check to make sure that the rounded edge of the worktop is on the left hand side.
5 – This is refered to as the front face of the cutting slot throughout this guide
6 – This is refered to the back face of the cutting slot throughout this guide
Once you have the worktop set up for your particular male joint and simiar to the above, check to make sure that the worktop is secure and that once you start routing there will be no obstructions as it is not good practice to stop the router midway through a cut.

Cutting male joints

The next stage is to cut the joint. Place the router at the position shown below and make sure the guide bush is between the cutting slot.

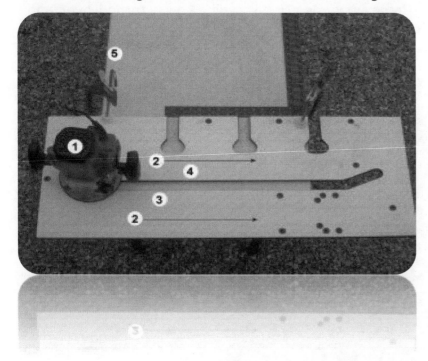

1 – Router
2 – Cutting direction
3 – Back face of cutting slot
4 – Front face of cutting slot
5 – Rounded Face of worktop

Set the router cutter to a depth of approximately 5mm for the first cut.
Start the router and guide it along the slot with the guide bush against the 'back face' of the cutting slot
Increase the depth of the cutter by 10 to 15mm* and make a second cut along the slot
Repeat the process until you have removed the waste completely
Set the router cutter to its maximum depth and make one final cut with the guide bush against the 'front face' of the cutting slot. This will remove the final 1mm and should leave a perfect cut joint
Inspect the cut for any damage – if need be you can reset the jig back 1 or 2mm and recut the joint to rectify any problems.
Once you are happy that the joint is cut correctly, remove the clamps and jigs and sand the newly cut edge with fine sandpaper to remove any loose particles of chipboard. Do not sand the laminate surface – it will scratch.
Put the worktop in a safe place until you are ready to cut the bolt recesses on the underside – see later in this guide.

* 15mm is the maximum recommended cut for a router. Depending on which router you have you may need to significantly reduce the depth of each cut. When cutting along the cutting slot the router should be manoeuvred with little energy – if you find you have to push hard to get the router to move you have either; set the cutter too deep or the blade is blunt or the router is underpowered.

Setting the jig to cut female joints

The layout below will cut a right hand female joint
To cut a left hand female joint the setup will be the same but the worktop will be turned over with the chipboard face upwards. The jig will also be turned over and the pegs placed in the same holes but from the otherside.
Female joints are always cut into the rounded edge and along the length of the worktop
See Diagram 1 to determine which joint you need to cut

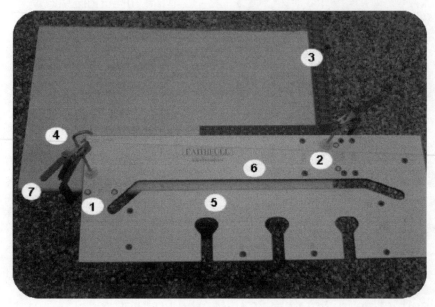

1 – Pegs
2 – Pegs
3 – Builders square
4 – Clamps
5 – Back face of cutting slot
6 – Front face of cutting slot
7 – Rounded edge

1 – Place 2 pegs in the holes as illustrated and usually marked 'F' for female – make sure the pegs are flush with the surface of the jig so that they do not interfere with the path of the router.
2 – Place 2 pegs in the relevant holes for the width of worktop you are cutting, i.e. 500mm, 600mm etc. Make sure the pegs are flush with the surface of the jig

3 - Position a builders square or similar tool along the side edge of the worktop to ensure the jig is at 90°

4 – Use 2 clamps to hold the jig to the worktop and workbenches making sure they will not be in the way once you start routing. If the worktop is a long length and supported by a workbench at the other end, apply another 2 clamps to that end.
5 – Front face of the cutting slot
6 – Back face of the cutting slot
7 – Rounded edge of worktop

Cutting female joints

The next stage is to cut the joint. Place the router at the position shown below and make sure the guide bush is between the cutting slot

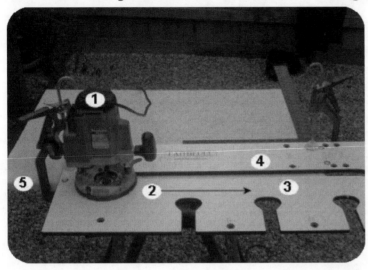

1 – Router in starting position
2 – Direction of cut
3 – Back face of cutting slot
4 – Front face of cutting slot
5 – Rounded edge of worktop

Set the router cutter to a depth of approximately 5mm for the first cut.
Start the router and guide it along the slot with the guide bush against the 'back face' of the cutting slot
Increase the depth of the cutter by 10 to 15mm* and make a second cut along the slot
Repeat the process until you have removed the waste completely
Set the router cutter to its maximum depth and make one final cut with the guide bush againt the 'front face' of the cutting slot. This will remove the final 1mm and should leave a perfect cut joint

Inspect the cut for any damage – you cannot reset this joint to make a deeper cut to rectify any mistakes or damage so use extreme care when cutting female joints.
Once you are happy that the joint is cut correctly, remove the clamps and jigs and sand the newly cut edge with fine sandpaper to remove any loose particles of chipboard. <u>Do not</u> sand the laminate surface – it will scratch.

Put the worktop in a safe place until you are ready to cut the bolt recesses on the underside – see later in this guide.

** 15mm is the maximum recommended cut for a router. Depending on which router you have you may need to significantly reduce the depth of each cut. When cutting along the cutting slot the router should be manoeuvred with little energy – if you find you have to push hard to get the router to move you have either; set the cutter too deep or the blade is blunt or the router is underpowered.

Setting the jig for bolt recesses

The layout below is to cut bolt recesses to a male joint

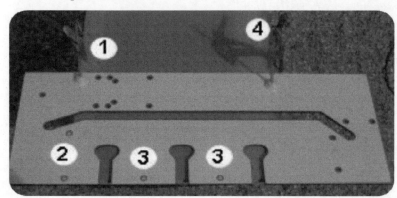

This worktop is upside down as all bolt recesses need to go on the underside

1 – Flat edge of worktop
2 – Pegs
3 – Pegs
4 – Rounded edge worktop

Place pegs in holes 2 &3, usually marked B for bolts.
Position the jig so that pegs 2 are butted against the straight side edge and pegs 3 are butted against the newly cut edge of the worktop.
If all 4 pegs are butted against the worktop the jig should automatically be square on the worktop. It is not important if the jig is slightly out of square but if it is obviously not square you will need to recheck the positioning.

The layout below is to cut bolt recesses to a female joint

This worktop is upside down as all bolt recesses need to go on the underside
1 – Pegs
2 – Pegs
3 – Rounded face of worktop
4 – Back edge of worktop

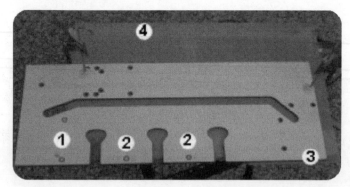

Place pegs in holes 1 &2, usually marked B for bolts.

Position the jig so that pegs 1 are butted against the straight side edge and pegs 2 are butted against the newly cut joint of the worktop.

If all 4 pegs are butted against the worktop the jig should automatically be square on the worktop. It is not important if the jig is slightly out of square but if it is obviously not square you will need to recheck the positioning.

Cutting bolt recesses

The picture below is the finished result after routing the bolt recesses.

To cut the recesses.
Set the cutter depth to approximately 20mm which should be sufficient for most joining bolts.
Starting with the first recess on the left, guide the router around the jig cut-out in a clockwise movement.
Make sure you remove all waste from the cut-out so that the base of the hole is flat and even.
Place a bolt in the first recess to check it sits either flush or just below the surface of the worktop, if the bolt sits above the surface adjust the router cutting depth.
Repeat the process for the other 2 recesses.
Remove the jig and clean out all sawdust from the recesses
Rub down any rough edges on the underside of the worktop with fine sandpaper

Before cutting the 2nd set of recesses for the opposite joint
Check that you have positioned the jig correctly and that the recesses on the 2nd worktop will line up with the first – this can be done using a tape measure.

Joining the worktops

The picture below shows the worktops turned upside down for clarity. When joining the worktops you will be in the cupboard underneath and some extra lighting will be useful.

Apply a thin coat of PVA adhesive to both faces of the join and allow it to dry – this is not to stick the worktops together but to prevent any moisture getting into the worktop

Place the worktops in position on the kitchen units and manoeuvre them so that the joint is as close to fitted as possible. Once you know the worktops will fit together and the bolt holes line up underneath you can apply colour fill to the worktop if required.

Put the bolts in the bolt holes from underneath and tighten them by hand until they stay in position.
Tighten each one little by little making sure the join stays perfect and both top surfaces are flush with each other. Wear safety glasses while doing this as if the bolts fall out they tend to fall into your face
If one surface protrudes above the other use an offcut of wood and a hammer to gently tap the two surfaces flush while tightening the bolts. You may have to repeat this several times until all bolts are tight and the surfaces are flush. Take care when using this method and never hit the offcut too hard as it could cause the laminate to chip.

Wipe excess of colour fill away as soon as possible using a soft cloth and the acetone supplied with it

The Finish

A good professional looking joint can be achieved following the procedures shown in this guide. Not all joints on all worktops can be invisible but you should be able to make them with no obvious gaps.

High gloss worktops are more difficult to disguise the joint line just by the nature of the gloss finish. Matt finished worktops of a dark colour are the easiest to make the joint 'invisible'

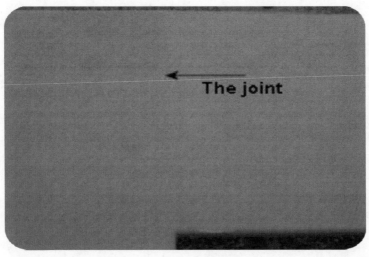

Once the joint is finished the worktops can be secured to the base units.

<u>Looking after the joints</u>

Although joints need no maintenance there are some things you can do to make sure the joint lasts as long as the kitchen does;

Don't put the kettle near the joint, keep water away from it and if you do spill some, wipe it up straight away

Corners are a favourite area for people to sit – try to dissuade them from sitting on joints

Comments or questions can be sent to SteveLake@diykitchenfitting.co.uk